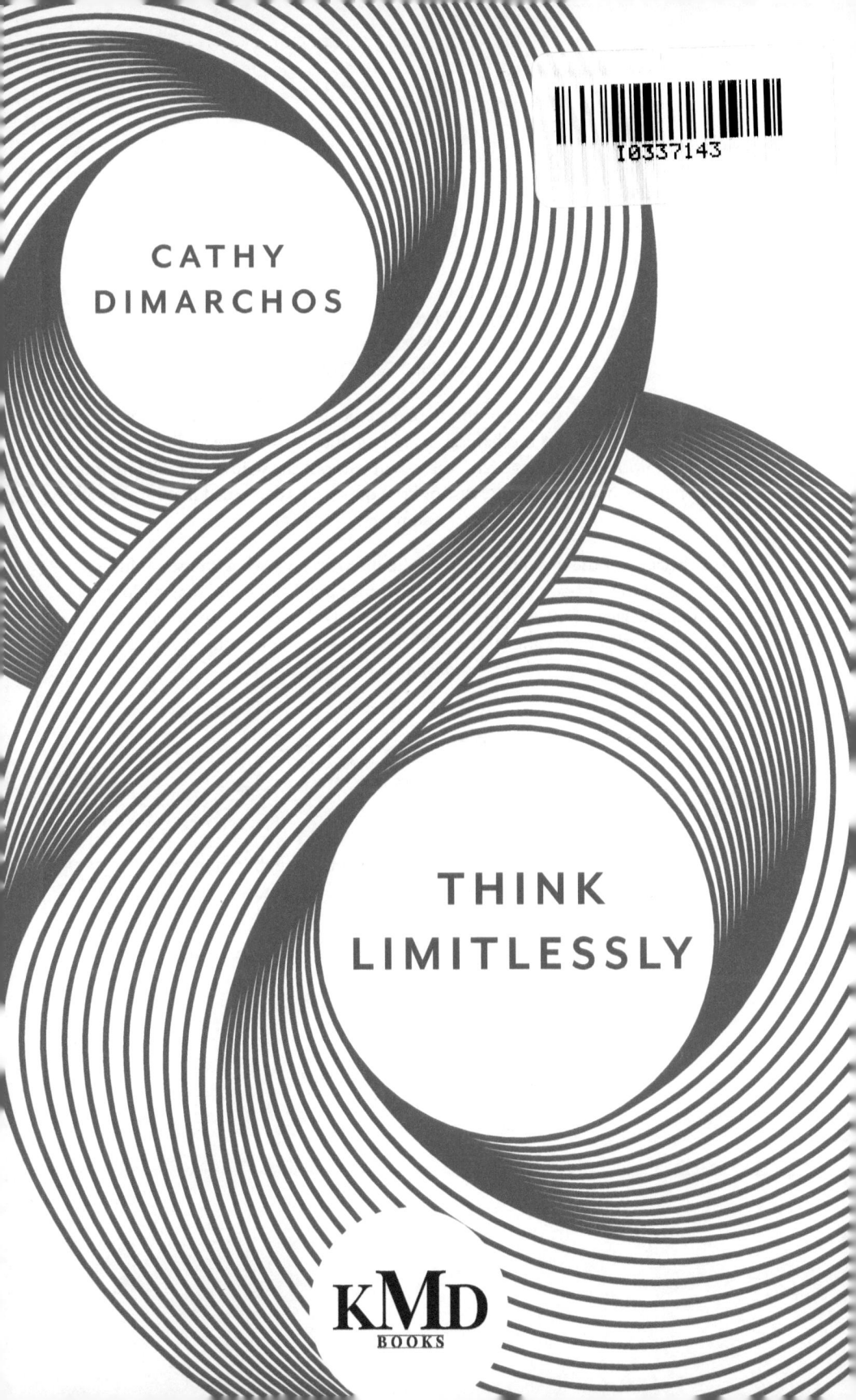

Copyright © Cathy Dimarchos
First published in Australia in 2022
by KMD Books
Waikiki, WA 6169

All rights reserved. No part of this book may be used or reproduced by any means, graphic, electronic, or mechanical, including photocopying, recording, taping or by any information storage retrieval system without the written permission of the copyright owner except in the case of brief quotations embodied in critical articles and reviews.

Because of the dynamic nature of the Internet, any web addresses or links contained in this book may have changed since publication and may no longer be vaild. The views expressed in this work are solely those of the author and do not necessarily reflect the views of the publisher and the publisher hereby disclaims any responsibility for them.

 A catalogue record for this work is available from the National Library of Australia

National Library of Australia Catalogue-in-Publication data:
Think Limitlessly/Cathy Dimarchos

ISBN: 978-0-6455691-7-9
(Hardback)

ISBN: 978-0-6455691-8-6
(Paperback)

ISBN: 978-0-6455691-9-3
(Ebook)

THIS BOOK PAYS IT FORWARD

through the Raise the Baseline Programs

The Raise the Baseline programs were established to support and develop future leaders globally with a focus on paying things forward in developing communities and countries. Our programs are designed to enable young people to become co-creators of the future, their own architect and help them discover that community is global.

Participants of our programs are from all walks of life, starting as young as twelve years of age through to young adults. We want them to be able to identify the things that they want for themselves and for the world as they step forward leading a life that they deserve. They each have their own vision of what success may look like and we want to encourage them to choose the path that will work for them. This means our role as leaders, parents, teachers and influencers is to enable them to see their own capabilities and strengths so that they can stay true to themselves.

The programs are focused around key milestones in their lives to leverage what they have already experienced and learnt and enable them to continue to grow and be confident with what they have done, where they have come from and most importantly where they want to go.

Having limitless beliefs and the ability to dream is in every child and that is what we want to cultivate whilst also developing an entrepreneurial mindset. Careers in the future will require agility, antifragility and skills that are transferable across the globe so that they can navigate from one job to another and not be tied down to any one location or pathway.

Theory-based roles will be a thing of the past and the workforce will be in demand of people that can bring their whole self to what they do, who can show they are conscious of themselves and of others and willing to make a global impact. Being able to think limitlessly and embrace failures as opportunities to learn and grow from the experience are the roots of an entrepreneurial mindset and essential to create, innovate and be able to find the solutions needed for tomorrow – their future.

Our children are stepping forward into an evolving and rapidly changing environment, one that we are only just beginning to understand. It is important that our actions of today are made to create impact for the future; focusing on survival only is not enough anymore, we need to build and thrive while taking others with us.

Collaboration and the art of embracing differences form part of the new way of thinking and living so they can be the leaders of tomorrow. Today is about gifting knowledge that we wish we had when we were younger, so that we could be courageous in the way we stepped into the world.

Giving them the things that we all desire most: a sense of purpose, belonging and the ability to create an impact that is greater than self. We all talk about finding our tribe, this is why our programs are about our children creating the tribe that brings them to a higher vibration. Success for our future generation looks different to ours and their path forward will be different.

Join me in developing our future generation for our children to be the architects that reshape a better tomorrow and the leaders that change the world.

If you would like to support your child to be a leader creating impact for tomorrow, register for them for one of our programs here: solutions2you.com.au/rais-the-baseline-academy

If you run a developing community project and would like to talk to us about how we might be able to help young leaders in your community please register your interest here: solutions2you.com.au/take-action

If you can help us create impact through government, education departments or policy, grants, communities and connections please connect with us here so we can create a ripple effect: solutions2you.com.au/donate-to-raise-the-baseline

FOREWORD

HE Dr Edna Joyce Santos MD, DPBO, SBO
Secretary-General, Royal Movement International Group
29 September 2022 UAE

When I was approached by Ms Cathy Dimarchos to write the foreword for her anthology, *Think Limitlessly,* I was delighted, awed, excited and privileged at the same time for she has created quite an impact globally. Cathy is an impeccable lady who is quite an enigma all by herself. After spending time with her, I learned about her story as she candidly discussed her passion in moulding the future generation in impoverished communities, especially in Africa, and most especially in motivating women to stand up for themselves and contribute towards a brighter tomorrow.

This anthology serves as a compendium of stories of people Cathy has successfully brought together to inspire others from all walks of life, to lift their vibrations and think beyond the self ... to *Think Limitlessly*. Sometimes they need to hear that they are not alone in their struggles and that there were people whose stories would resonate with them.

I highly recommend this anthology and I am looking forward for more inspiring books from my phenomenal friend, Ms Cathy Dimarchos.

INTRODUCTION

I have often shared that people are at the centre of everything we do. No matter where you are, where you were born or where you choose to live your life, the choices you make will impact people and create a ripple. It will create an impact that reverberates out and then bounces back with universal feedback.

Being prepared to live life and to have joy is what enables us to live to our greatest potential, and this then enables us to THINK LIMITLLESLY. There are no barriers that hold us back except for those we create for ourselves. So, as you begin to read the stories of these incredible authors, know that you can create a future for yourself that includes all that you dare to dream.

'Be comfortable with being uncomfortable; this is how we grow.' – Cathy Dimarchos

CONTENTS

CATHY DIMARCHOS
THE AWAKENED MIND 1

DANIELLE LOADER
LIFE BEGINS AT THE END OF YOUR COMFORT ZONE 16

EMMA WEAVER
BE ALL THAT YOU ARE TO BECOME ALL THAT YOU CAN BE 38

HAZEL HERRINGTON
LIMITLESS: THINK GLOBAL 55

KAREN MC DERMOTT
AWAKEN YOUR POTENTIAL 72

LEANNE MURNER
WHAT LIGHTS YOU UP 83

OKSANA KUKURUDZA
LIKE MOTHER, LIKE DAUGHTER 98

THERESA HAENN
SETTLING INTO MYSELF AND MY PURPOSE 117

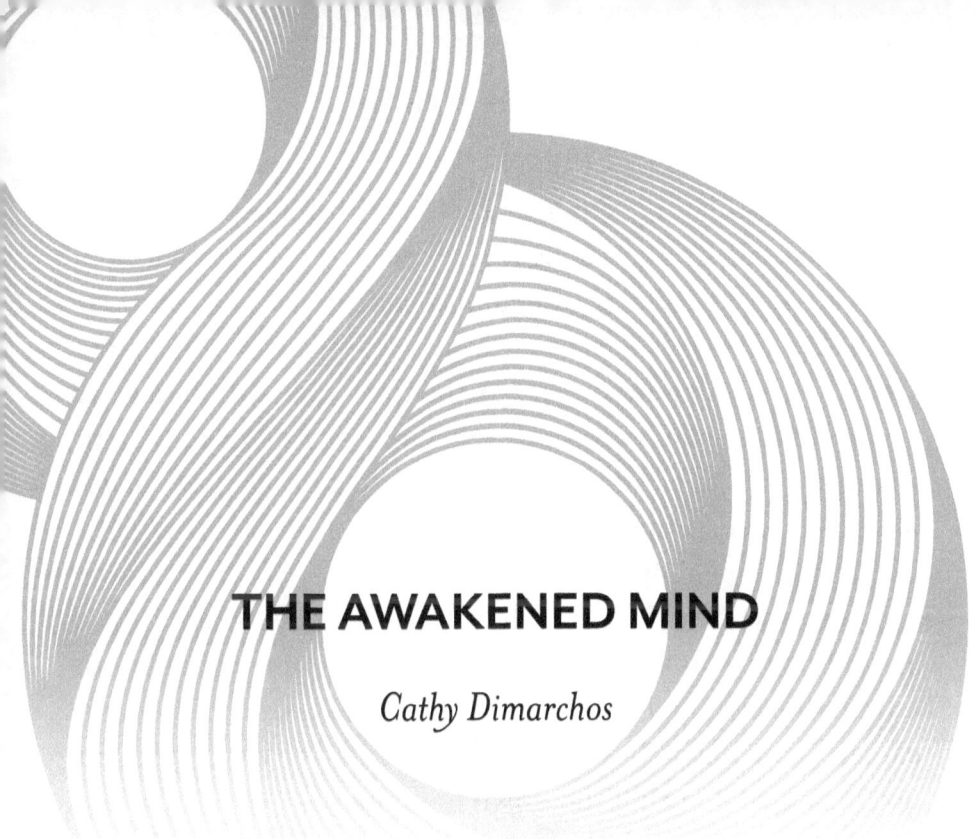

THE AWAKENED MIND

Cathy Dimarchos

It's Friday the thirteenth 2019, and I am on a flight back home to Sydney, New South Wales, from Perth, Western Australia, after a national speaking engagement on 'change and transformation' with business owners and industry leaders. I was thinking about an ophthalmologist appointment I had for my father that following Wednesday and how he would be discharged from hospital on the Tuesday (he had been admitted to hospital whilst I was travelling but was recovering in time to be discharged the day before so we could make that appointment). Little did I know then that some four days later he would have a tragic fall that would change everything. We live life with the understanding that we know what we know, and that is what we plan for – I now call this 'sleepwalking through life'. There is so much more that we can do, and it's not just about being 'conscious', it's about being 'intentionally conscious', and this makes a difference.

It was Tuesday 17 March at 10:45am when I receive a phone call saying, 'Cathy, I'm calling from Shell Harbour Hospital, your mum is with the social worker and is in a bit of shock, your dad has had a fall and is not well, can you make it to the hospital?' I was in a meeting in the city at the time with someone I had known professionally for some years, and as I sat there looking into Lee's eyes, a sickening feeling poured over me. *Why is my mum with a social worker? How serious is this?* So many questions ran through my mind.

'Yes, of course, but what has happened? Let Mum know I am on my way. It will take me about two hours to get there as I am in the city, and I will need to go home first to pick up the car and drive down.' It was a fresh day, and whilst the wind was not strong, I felt a chill run down my spine.

There was so much that I was trying to process and the one thing that kept repeating on me was that there was a social worker with Mum, and they suggested that I not delay. As I looked at Lee and explained, I recall seeing the softening in his eyes – he had felt this type of pain himself, he had cared for his mother and had shared some of his challenges with me. I excused myself and began to call my family to make them aware of what seemed to be a severe situation.

I am sure, like me, you too have a memory in your life where things become surreal, so much so that in that split second you realise how truly precious life is. That day was one of those for me, as was the moment I sat by my father's bed, three days later, realising that life would never be the same again. I held his hand in mine knowing he was slipping away. I also had my mother collapse on me in the car with heart failure, now needing to be admitted to another hospital to be treated by a cardiac team.

Life takes a turn in seconds, and it is the choices we make in those moments that show us who we are as humans and who we choose to be. It is in these moments we can become acutely awake, or we can continue to sleepwalk through life believing we are contributing, but in reality, we contribute only to self. We are custodians of this world and are placed here to contribute to others before self, but so seldom do our actions reflect this.

I have lived a comfortable life, one that I would say is privileged, having had opportunities to travel, see the world and experience different cultures. I have had life-changing experiences through volunteering in impoverished communities, but nothing prepared me for what I was about to experience. I thought I had become more awake in life some five years earlier, when I first travelled to Africa, but I was yet to truly understand what being awake was.

You see, in 2014, I followed my then-seventeen-year-old daughter to Tanzania. She had decided that as she had finished school, she would volunteer there for three months in a community where she could make a difference. 'I want to make a real difference. Everyone else wants to go to Canada, Fiji or the USA, but I want to go somewhere where they really need help.' How can you deny a child with such a vision the opportunity to follow their dream? To think limitlessly and selflessly? So, we made it happen.

Whilst there is so much that I can share about that trip, I will focus on what began to be my path to becoming awake in life. We spent time living with the Maasai in Endulen, Ngorongoro, Tanzania, and here I began to see my own subconscious bias, my limitations, and all whilst I could see that I could also create change and be part of the positive impact for humanity that I so wanted for the world.

It's not that unusual that we really begin to understand things through lived experience, but at times even that is not enough as we tend to default to what's comfortable, what's safe and what's known. There were many things that I realised not only about myself on that trip, but I also recognised that as one individual I could create a ripple effect, and that ripple can impact others to do the same.

My daughter began that ripple with her vision of who she wanted to support and why it was important to stretch outside of her comfort, which led to me to follow her. These trips then continued over the years, with me taking other family members and friends, which then led to the development of leadership programs for children and aspiring entrepreneurs.

So, on that day, while I sat wondering what life would be like for me without my father and my mother still laying in hospital in critical condition whilst Australia was in full lockdown with the pandemic, I realised something. *This is my time to do more and to be more.*

It's strange how in moments of crisis, I tend to have the clearest of visions. It's almost like I can slow down time, it's like being in the *Matrix* movie, watching things in slow motion but being able to see light-years ahead, all at the same time. I hit my 'reset button' that day. I knew that the world was shutting down around me with the pandemic, but I was also intentionally conscious that my personal world would take another turn. My father's fate was known, but my mother was still on tenderhooks – either way, my road forward was not going to be life like I had known it, but this was my opportunity to choose who I wanted to be and the impact I wanted to make.

I knew that the world's state of uncertainty would have a greater impact on those in developing countries and would bring about greater division between those who live a life of privilege and those who barely survive. We all know that for change to occur in the future we need to do things differently today, and I wanted to do my part.

I reached out to Helen in Tanzania – whom I had developed a wonderful relationship with and had been working with since we first met in 2014 – initially to see what the impact was with the pandemic there, but then to share my vision on supporting aspiring leaders who wanted to also pay things forward, become entrepreneurs or lead with influence and shape a better tomorrow. Together, we ran master classes and Q&As across continents, and then I realised I could do more.

With over three decades of experience in finance and having set up several businesses since 1997, I knew that my lived experiences and knowledge, if shared, could create a greater ripple especially if I incorporated qualifications as a counsellor. I explored changing some of the training and work I had done for adults and simplifying them so that we could begin to educate children so that they could imbed practices from a young age that would enable them to think about the future with a different lens.

The one thing I have learnt in life is that if you want to see change, you need to be part of the change. So, here I was, beginning to see the change that I wanted to contribute to. I needed to be at the core so I could create a ripple that would then reverberate a positive impact on the world.

The second thing I realised was that, no matter who you are, what line of work you are in (self-employed or an employee) you can lead, but first you must learn to lead yourself. Once you understood that, it was then your obligation to show others how they can do it too. You see, true leaders develop more leaders, and there are always more people to develop. They don't seek to be influencers, they seek to influence for purpose and for impact that elevates others and not themselves.

The more I thought about it, the more I realised I could do that, but I also realised that if I could shape the mind of a child, we really could accelerate change for humanity at a faster trajectory, especially if we imbedded the gift of paying things forward as a lived practice.

It was like, the more AWAKE I became, the more I realised I needed to do more, but with this came other considerations. When we add things into our lives, we must also let other things go. Yes, we need to make choices about what we want in life, just as much as what we don't. We need to have alignment in everything we do, and we need to be consistent.

I knew most of these things, but here is how I began to realise that we may all be aware of these things but seldom put them into place. We continue to live on autopilot, sleepwalking through life. You see, knowing something and doing something about it are two very different things. To create a positive impact is another layer. We first need to choose to be awake and then we need to action what we know. Without the action, nothing changes. Without intentional consciousness we seek for self not for others.

I also realised that showing others step by step how to do something was the key to creating a greater ripple, so being comfortable to take others on the journey with you, openly and freely, whilst scary at times, is the only way to build trust and to make people feel like they belong. Better yet, it enables them to know that they can do it too.

I have reflected a great deal in life, especially over the past seven years, and I keep reminding myself of how much more there is yet to learn, but if I continue to focus on humanity, the planet and everything in it will vibrate at a higher level. I will continue to make the positive impact that is much needed for our future generation. I see life as my obligation to leave things in a better place than where things are today.

I see our future as a place where we live more awake and intentionally conscious of others, and we know how we want to contribute so that we create a positive impact. So often I hear people say, 'I would love to do that,' but that is where it stops. It isn't because they lost passion, or that they were just giving 'lip service', it is usually because they didn't know where to begin. People, in general, want to contribute to something bigger than themselves, but the one thing that holds them back – no matter what it is – is not knowing where to start.

This is why it's so important to take people on a journey with us. This is where real impact begins. When we contribute to something greater than ourselves, we have a sense of purpose, we feel like we belong and most importantly we show others how they can do it too. All of these require us to pause and to be intentionally conscious about the choices that we make, which leads me to influence.

As we continue to evolve and communicate through social media, we also have the ability to be an influencer or to influence. I, for one, am very conscious of what the differences are and who I choose to be. For clarity, influencing for impact is about supporting and elevating others. Being an influencer is about self-promotion – so I am conscious of the way I communicate and the impact I choose to make. I am also conscious of the balance that is possible when you combine both.

Today, I know where I want to be in five years from now and how I will live out my life. I see the red earth under my feet, I feel the warmth of the sun and the light rain as it falls in the middle of the day. I hear the joyful voices of children who feel hope and inspiration for what's to come and I see a planet that is beginning to rejuvenate because we as humans have become more awake in life knowing that we can all contribute to something greater than ourselves.

The journey that once was engulfed by a 'chasing game' is now one where I pause and listen to better understand. I plan to respond rather than react. I live not for today but for our grandchildren's grandchildren because they matter and the choices we make today will shape tomorrow.

Africa may be where I started my awakening moments, but I am not naive to know that I don't know it all. I search out like-minded people across the globe, knowing that as our paths cross, it will bring us together to create a greater trajectory that raises the baseline of where people begin life, especially those in developing countries.

Now that you know where I will be in years to come, where do you think you might be? Better still, where do you choose to be? Who will be on the journey with you, and will you be an influencer or a person of influence?

Will you think limitlessly? Will you navigate through life on autopilot, or have you heard my calling, 'Don't sleepwalk through life'?

People call me an idealist
Knowing the impact you want to make in life and who you choose to be is not easy. I keep refining this. There is no label, not where I sit, but drawing a line in the sand and defining who you choose to be and how you want to create greater impact is the beginning. For me, it began in the middle of Ngorongoro, Tanzania, as I began to understand there was so much more that I didn't know. There was so much more that I needed to be conscious of within myself and others, but it wasn't until I lost my father that

I realised how precious life was and there was so much more that I could do than think about myself.

It's funny how it sometimes takes one thing to create that awakening moment in life that gives us a nudge and asks us what we truly want to do. Today, my vision is global, and it's beyond me. In many ways, there will be things that will occur that will be beyond my lifetime, but that is what life is about. Not to leave things behind, but to pay it forward so that our future generations live a life that they deserve. A life where we walk the planet aligned in values and beliefs. A life where we have equality, compassion and the ability to be beyond resilient – to be antifragile so that we learn from what has failed us and then strengthen from it.

Easy is an option
Life throws curveballs all the time; we can choose to swerve and let them go past so we don't get hurt, or we can be intentional and stand our ground, focused, so we can catch them. We can stand still, and it will hit us and possibly cause pain, but it's the lessons that we take away from each of these that will allow us to learn, develop and do something different the next time around.

I have often shared that obstacles are a way of showing us that there is another solution somewhere, we just need to change the lens through which we see things. When we are prepared to stay in pursuit of what is important, we will achieve the impossible.

This is how we develop a limitless belief.

Creating the road map
Our future generations have inspired me. As I listen to their conversations, I hear them talk about global issues at the age of ten and twelve and wonder how to foster this. As a child, I don't recall having these types of discussions, so rather than ignoring

them, I ask more questions so I can better understand what is important to them. If they have the ability and intuition to think beyond self, then we can contribute by enabling them to be contributors to the solution.

The future is theirs, even more so than mine, so knowing how I might be able to contribute with tangible tools, skills and insight will ensure we expedite the trajectory forward. Don't be the person who told you to play small or that you could not do something. Be the person who encourages and then takes that one step further to help them achieve what may have seemed impossible.

Be consciously awake
Today it is 'think limitlessly', but tomorrow it will be 'collaborations for global impact'! I travel the world again, but now I pause to better understand who crosses my path, what they are in search of and how I may connect people who look to contribute to shaping a better tomorrow.

I listen to what is not said, just as much as what is said, because that is where we begin to truly recognise who we are in the presence of. I say no to things more than I say yes because I am consciously awake and know the impact I want to make in the world. As people around me learn the art of speaking, I continue to develop the art of listening.

I choose to go against the grain, challenging pathways as it breaks through barriers to create new beginnings that bring about innovation and change. Of course, there is fear at times, for it is the unknown that frightens us, but when we see a future that is filled with joy, equality and a life that is lived with values, you know that every difficult moment has been worth the angst, sleepless nights and frustrations that you have faced.

No matter what your journey is in life, know that you always have choice. A choice to leave behind what is not serving you. Choice in who you choose to be. Choice in responding or reacting and a choice in what ripple you create.

My journey forward is to create economic security for those who don't have a voice, don't have access and don't have influence yet. Education sits at the core of everything, and how we make people feel will either enable them to be part of the change or cripple them.

We are living in a cosmic cycle where the choices we make will either create greater division for humanity or bring us closer together. I know the path that I choose, now it's up to you which path you take, and staying silent is as equally powerful as creating division.

Developing future leaders and an entrepreneurial mindset is the path that I choose, and when aligned with values and a practice to pay things forward, I am hopeful that the ripple I create is one that bounces back with positive universal feedback.

Today it's Tanzania, tomorrow it may be Nigeria or Columbia or Haiti. The place is not what will be important, but the number of people that will be on the journey with me will. As each child completes one of our programs, they gain more insight on who they can be. They develop greater leadership skills and stronger communication skills, and most importantly, they look at the world as their community and they better understand how they can be contributors to shaping a better tomorrow.

With each business client I provide advice to, or with each executive I coach or mentor, I show them the power they have to influence for impact.

You have not chosen to read this book by chance. You have been drawn to my vision, the stories and the impact that this book is making, and as you read through this chapter and that of the other co-authors, you also have discovered your passion to do things differently, to think BIGGER and to THINK LIMITLESSLY.

If you want to know where to start your journey then reach out, connect, follow or join me on my journey. My book is in your hands, this is not by chance. This is where I pause, reflect and listen to better understand. Looking inward, you do have the answers, you just need to give yourself permission to step outside of your lane and go against the grain. As you do things, know that you are being intentionally conscious and you have chosen to no longer sleepwalk through life.

CATHY DIMARCHOS

Cathy is an unstoppable global award-winning business advisor and mentor to people who influence. She is a humanitarian, two-time TedX speaker and award-winning author who is focused on creating IMPACT. She works with ethical conscious leaders and elevates them to think BIGGER. Her legacy is to elevate humanity consciously.

Her values take centrestage and business becomes honest and expressive as she helps people be comfortable with being uncomfortable, unlearn patterns that don't serve them and helps them step forward with clarity that will enable them to reach their goals.

With empathy and strategic positioning, she empowers people to establish healthy professional boundaries, think limitlessly and challenge norms, whilst rediscovering a curiosity of knowledge and themselves.

Website: solutions2you.com.au
Instagram: @cathydimarchos & @solutions2you_consulting
Linkedin: Cathy Dimarchos & Solutions2You Pty Ltd
TikTok: cathy_dimarchos
Facebook: Cathy Dimarchos – Mentor and Coach at Solutions2You

TOP TAKEAWAY TIPS

- Choose to be intentionally conscious so that as you live life, you make choices that will create greater impact for those around you.

- Choose to be a person of influence and enable others to influence but not to be an influencer that self-promotes and gains.

- Transparency is key. It's what you don't say that holds the truth, not want you say so that people can hear.

- Be more than resilient, become antifragile, so that you strengthen from what you have experienced.

- Being conscious and having purpose alone are not enough. Being intentionally conscious and being purposeful to create impact for others is where you begin.

LIFE BEGINS AT THE END OF YOUR COMFORT ZONE

Danielle Loader

Some days I still feel like pinching myself when I reflect on how far I have come. Now a global business owner living in Australia, married to my 'lobster' (my forever, lobsters mate for life), mum of two amazing young sons – it is a far cry from the local council estate I grew up on in the south-east of England.

Life has been a roller-coaster is an understatement, but through the highs and lows, happiness and pain, success and mistakes, love and loss, valuable lessons have been learnt along the way, even if I didn't know it at the time.

My mum pushed my brother, David, and me to always work hard and aspire for more. She raised the two of us on her own, sent us to schools out of area to give us a better education and worked three jobs to support us. David and I became entreprenurial from an early age, coming up with ideas to make our own pocket money which was handed to our friends without them giving it a second thought.

Wanting to keep up with our peers and not wanting to miss out, we would think of ideas to make some extra money. These included knocking on doors in our local neighbourhood offering to wash people's cars, providing gardening services and signing up to numerous paper rounds – hard work, determination and thinking outside of the box was ingrained in us from an early age.

At twenty-one, I lost my best friend to cancer. Experiencing loss and heartbreak for the first time, I remember the pain, hurt, anger and lost feeling so well. I went to stay with my grandma in Norfolk to get away and cried for a week. Every day, I would walk her dog along the beach without a soul in sight. I'd sit and watch the waves of the ocean wash in and out – it's like they were soothing and healing my mind. After a week, I vividly remember watching the waves and seeing two paths, with two choices ahead of me. On one path I remain sad and angry and live in the mindset that life was not fair, or I could be thankful for the time I had with Kerry and grateful for the opportunities I had ahead of me, by making the most of the life I was blessed to have been given.

I decided to take the second path and came back home with a sense of determination and fight, wanting to make my life count and not just cruise through it with the hand I was dealt with. To this day, I still think of my dear friend, and if I'm having a low period, a lull or a sense of self-pity, I give myself some tough love and snap out of it because I am lucky to be here to experience it – Kerry was taken way too young.

At twenty-two, I moved to London to study at the University of Westminster. I had also applied for the local University of Portsmouth. I remember the tough decision of choosing between the two. My heart was at home, but once I had been accepted into Westminster, I couldn't turn it down. London offered so much opportunity.

The first six months in London were tough; I was out of my comfort zone and felt very much a small fish in a very big pond. With support and encouragement from Mum and David, it was one of my best decisions in life. It was the start of a new identify for me and making it on my own.

Sadly, my dad passed away during my final exams at university. He wasn't around when David and I were growing up, but I reached out to him when I was fifteen and we developed a close bond and friendship. I was very sad to have lost Dad, but I remember my biggest fear being that I was going to shatter like I had when I lost Kerry.

The mind is such a powerful thing; understanding yourself and finding inner peace is such an important step to take throughout your life. Even if others don't understand you, take the time to understand yourself. We all heal and deal with things in different ways. Through my life, it is during the pain and tough times that my focus and determination really kicks in.

If anything, losing Dad ignited a strength within me, and I stayed in control. 'It's not what happens to you, but how you react to it that matters,' said Epictetus. I wrote a poem and read it at my dad's funeral, promising to work hard and make him proud.

After university, I was successful in a graduate placement for a national newspaper as a recruitment sales executive. There were over four hundred applications and only ten places, so receiving the call I had been successful was mind-blowing. This gave me the confidence and belief in myself that I could stand out and with hard work and a positive mindset I could achieve what I set my mind to.

In this role, I developed my relationship management and communication skills in a target-driven environment, which I thrived in. I found my superpower of connecting easily with people, developing and maintaining relationships, through offering tailored campaigns, solutions and a first-class client service.

Our superpower is our own particular genius. I took mine for granted for many years, as many people do. By continuously developing and strengthening our superpower, we have the possibility of achieving extraordinary results and it allows us the greatest opportunity for success.

Have you identified your superpower? Do you maximise it in business and your career? This really is a powerful tool; identifying your superpower will bring you a limitless approach to business and life and maximise success.

Through the power of connection, I was referred for a position in a successful recruitment agency. This is where my agency recruitment career started, where I could maximise and develop my love and passion for people by helping them find a new job or career. My motto 'changing lives' was born, along with a dream of becoming a successful agency recruiter and maximising the London market.

At twenty-five, recruiting and appointing people in senior accounting and financial services positions, I had massive imposter syndrome and I definitely faked it until I made it. I then moved into the professional and business support market – here I was in my element. I excelled in matching candidates and clients more on culture fit than skill set, which came easier to me through reading people and connecting easily with many different people at different levels.

Working for nearly ten years in the London job market, I worked for global companies, exceeded targets and won awards. This led to me being headhunted for a role at a leading Australian recruitment firm, relocating me and providing sponsorship in a very desired market.

In 2011, I was at a crossroads in my life when this opportunity knocked. Many of my friends were settling down, having children, and the expectation at my age was that I should too, but I was not going to settle for anything but butterflies.

Packing up my life into two suitcases at the age of thirty-three, I took the leap of faith and relocated to the other side of the world. With a two-year plan, little did I know I would meet my now-husband, Matt, two weeks after arriving, call Australia my permanent home and raise my own family there. Life definitely does begin at the end of your comfort zone!

Starting out in a new market and country, the recruitment industry globally is known for being cutthroat, with high targets and high stress. Pre-pandemic, there was no flexibility to work from home, and hours were long.

Sadly, we lost Mum to breast cancer in 2015 at the age of sixty-four, when my first son Ollie just turned one. Mum was my best friend and biggest cheerleader. She had always thought limitlessly for David and me, supporting and pushing our dreams, but was so selfless and gracious along the way. She could have easily lived a life of resentment. Leaving an unhappy and destructive marriage with two young children in what felt like the middle of the night, starting life from scratch again and raising us on her own, she never complained. Mum worked three jobs across six days a week to support us, she was exhausted but always had a sense of pride and taught me the importance of independence. Being diagnosed the first time with breast cancer in her late fifties, she worked constantly through her treatment, travelling an hour on the train each way daily and hardly ever taking a sick day. To then be diagnosed terminal after being in complete remission for two years, life could have seemed unfair, but she held no grudges or bitterness and was humble and positive until the end. We shared her last weeks together; she confided in me she had no regrets in her life and reminded me to never sacrifice happiness. She made some tough decisions along the way, but to part this earth with no regrets is truly commendable, and she remains my inspiration.

Mum was loved by many, with over three hundred people attending the memorial service. Many business books encourage you to determine your why and ask you to question what legacy you want to leave behind. Mum left a lasting footprint on those whose lives she touched – unassumingly and by just being her. I want to do that and more, I want to make a difference and a positive impact to as many people as possible. There are many ways we can all 'change lives' and have a positive impact.

Returning to full-time work after maternity leave at a startup agency, I was soon back in the high stress of recruitment. After having our second son Harrison two years later, unfortunately things were not the same. My passion for managing, recruiting and 'changing lives', had been dulled by a toxic work culture and minimal flexibility, juggling a full-time job, baby and toddler with no local family support was tough.

Recruiting in the business support space, specialising in executive assistants, I spoke to amazing and talented EAs and office/business managers daily. Many had to compromise their roles and really push for the flexibility to have a day from home or adjust hours around day care and school pick-ups.

My experience in agency recruitment was that many consultants burnout by their forties, with a high percentage going internal into companies or choosing another career path, without any targets and the same monthly grind. It is instilled into you as an agency recruiter that you are only as good as your last month, so the pressure is constant, one month of not hitting targets can really take a toll on your confidence, productivity and results.

Mental health was a taboo subject back then. Many managers and colleagues over my twenty years in agency recruitment have struggled with mental health issues and stress, experienced burn-out and lost their spark and passion. It was time to take action to save mine and carve out my next chapter.

In January 2020, believing in myself and taking the leap of faith, I became co-owner of We Recruit. Group, setting up the We Recruit. Executive Support division from scratch.

I wanted to make a difference and still do the job I loved, being hands-on with recruitment and 'changing lives'. I wrote my business plan for the We Recruit. Executive Support division and determined my why. Within the business, I wanted to offer flexibility for team members to work from home and so they could have a healthy balance between work and family. I looked at my business why but also my personal one too. I did this so I would not lose focus on one and give them both the dedication required to have a healthy work-life balance, be successful in both areas, maximise my life and happiness and promote this across the team culture too.

My why is that I want to provide an expert recruitment service utilising, maximising and continuously developing my relationships, network and connections. To be hands-on and live my passion of helping people 'changing lives', through placing them in new opportunities, training, mentoring or paying it forward.

I want to have a team that's inspiring, passionate and loves what they do, whilst giving them the flexibility to be with their families and offer balance.

I want to use our skills, talent and networks to help people where we can. All whilst embracing change where required, pushing my boundaries but still having a balance and positive mindset. I want to be present and maximise the time spent with my husband and children, whilst practicing gratitude and enjoying the simple things in life with smiles and laughter.

We change when we become parents, our maternal instinct kicks in and many sacrifice work for home life or vice versa. I was determined to try and have the best of both worlds and help others do it too.

Raring to go and excited by the future, nothing could prepare us for the global pandemic that hit two months after the launch of our new business in March 2020. With recruitment freezes across all industries and divisions globally, no-one knew how long this would last and the impact it would have on people and business.

In true 'Danielle' survival mode, focus and determination comes from pain and uncertainty. It was scary at the time thinking my dream was over before it had begun, but little did I know the pandemic would be a new beginning for me.

The pandemic forced me to pause. No matter how much business development I did, it had no impact because no-one was hiring. Instead, I turned my focus on candidates – these were people who were really struggling. Being in the Sydney market for nearly ten years, I already had an extensive network, people were reaching out to me for help and advice, but with no active roles I became a sounding board for them and a support. I would spend up to an hour on the phone listening to some people who were really struggling with the market, their morale and their mental health was being compromised. Their job application was one in over four hundred, they would apply for over thirty jobs a day and not hear anything back, their confidence was on the floor. These candidates were amazing executive assistants and office managers, had exceptional backgrounds and were really suffering.

I partnered with a leading recruitment expert, Penny, who

has run her own amazing executive support agency for over twenty-five years. Together, we started hosting monthly virtual group training sessions, bringing people together, coaching them on interview, job application advice, how to maximise your CV and LinkedIn profile and EQ training. These groups started with eight people and were soon in double figures.

With a sense of purpose and a real passion to make a difference by helping people by paying it forward, we were all each other's therapist, in a way, and the support really helped. I started reaching out to mental health experts, EA mentors and motivational coaches, asking them to collaborate and host a 'Virtual Coffee & Learn' session with us.

We continue these to this day, hosting international speakers and getting up to triple figures in interest. The majority of attendees now are not active in the job market but looking to learn and be part of a community – by paying it forward and offering support, we changed many lives through the pandemic and continue to this day.

I thought of other ideas of how we could use our time and skills to pay it forward through the pandemic. I founded a volunteer group of like-minded and very talented women – WR Angels was born. We volunteered our time and donated resources to help local charities and people in need. We helped families and victims of domestic violence, underprivileged children, working mums juggling homeschooling and work through the pandemic and charities close to our heart, and continue to make a difference.

Giving is a powerful gift; ultimately, the person paying it forward grows as much as the person receiving the act of kindness. The pause through the pandemic opened my eyes wide to this, and as a company, group and family we look at ways to pay it forward whenever we can.

From our extended networks and community, we get many candidates and clients referred to us – the power of connection is a very strong thing. Finding a tribe is important – push yourself outside of your comfort zone and continue to connect with new people regularly. The butterfly effect is a powerful one and has massive impact. For me to even be writing this chapter is quite unbelievable, and it came from a chain of events that started two years ago. Don't take anything for granted; the world's opportunities are limitless, you just need to be there to grab them.

Coming out of the pandemic, we had big plans and have continued to dream big. Key achievements include being a finalist for Business Excellence in 2022, being identified as a Top 10 Talent Management Agency to Watch in 2022 by *The Australian Business Journal* as well as a finalist in AusMumpreneur for the Emerging Entrepreneur Award in 2021. Launching into the UK market in 2022, co-authoring a number-one Amazon bestselling business book with twenty-three amazing women in business, record months of billing and plans to launch into the US market, offering a business model like no other, our dream is to be recognised as the world's leading recruitment partner program. This was all achieved within our first three years of business, surviving a global pandemic and pivoting when needed. More importantly, to me, is the lives we have changed along the way, through many channels, including our Virtual Coffee & Learns and WR Angels projects. Many changed lives we will not even know about and the impact we have made. The smallest ripple can have a big impact in years to come.

If we can do this, so can you. Live your dreams, they are possible with the right planning, passion and resilience.

Leap of faith

I am always the person to chase the Yahtzee, rather than settle for threes.

Looking back, I held the power to make things possible from an early age. I hold Mum in high regard influencing this, she was a survivor and always thought limitlessly and believed in us.

A stereotype for my background was that I would not go to University, instead work in a low-paid job, remain in a working-class lifestyle and end up with a man like my father and likely be a single mum. I remember being so frustrated, angry and even scared by the stereotype that I would fall under; from this point I was determined to prove it wrong.

Unfortunately, through my teens I suffered class discrimination. With Mum sending us to a good school out of area, we were the common kids, and the posh kids in our neighbourhood singled us out on our walk home from the train station, with name-calling and even David being in a brawl – targeted by a group of bullies because we were different.

Thinking limitlessly, to me, is always believing you can do anything you set your mind to. With a positive mindset, passion and determination, you can break stereotypes, discrimination and make a change. Negativity breeds, cut it out and walk away from it where you can. Inner peace and a strong mind are essential – mental health is wealth, you must look after yourself along the way.

Becoming a mother and wanting to show my children the right path with no prejudice and discrimination also drives me – we really can change the world with kindness and acceptance starting at an early age.

Pivoting is key

Navigating through challenges in life has been a learning curve. Over the years, pain and loss have driven focus and determination.

I am a very passionate person. I am passionate about my work, family and friends. With passion comes emotion, and through some tough lessons, I have had to learn to take the emotion out, especially when it comes to friends and business.

I have led with my heart when people have suggested I should lead with my head. Some decisions and people have caused disappointment. People I have worked with and even hired into my business, who I thought were friends, didn't hold the same values as me. Trust and respect were broken, but after some tough lessons, I now take off my rose-tinted glasses, stop making excuses for people and see things for what they are. I'm still not sure if it's a strength or weakness of mine, but if trust and respect are compromised, I now move on. Once I have moved on, I don't look back or harbour negative emotions; I reset and move forward.

When making decisions, it is important to not make the same mistake twice – mistakes are lessons learnt. Really evaluate these lessons along the way and pass on knowledge and experience where you can. We can learn from ours but also other people's failures, so be wise.

Knowing your why and the type of person, manager, mentor or leader you want to be is important. Think about people that inspire you and who you aspire to be. Also giving time to understand who you don't want to be will give you a clear guideline, so you can set goals that will lead you on the right path.

Finding your tribe and people whose opinions you respect is important. Make sure you listen to the right people and let your ego go when needed. You can be passionate and always think you are right at the time you present your ideas, but on the occasions you are not right, it is important to recognise this. Time is not wasted on wrong ideas, these are lessons, but time and money can be wasted on egos and the point of proving you are right for the sake of it. Always be humble and self-aware.

Remember, plans don't always go to plan, and I have learnt this the hard way. The recruitment industry is heavily driven by the economic climate – I have been through recessions and a global pandemic. The quicker you can pivot or scale back when needed, the more resilient and successful you will be. There are always going to be things that happen that are out of your control, so don't be consumed by them. Get inner peace, think outside the box, pivot, replan and don't look back.

Always believe
Coming from a working-class background, I had to work hard to get to where I am, but I broke the stereotype by going to college, then onto university. The future generations can break down stereotypes and discrimination, one person at a time.

Tips I would give is to not conform to a stereotype, always believe you can be whoever and whatever you want to be. Dream big and don't settle for the norm.

Education is key, don't take school life and learning for granted, respect this from an early age, and from your experiences, find your passion and drive. Keep learning and developing, pushing yourself out of your comfort zone. By identifying your superpower and continuing to build on this, you will maximise your potential and success.

Unfortunately, there will always be challenges along the way, but no matter what your background is, a good work ethic and discipline can be embraced from an early age. Admiral William H McRaven, a Navy Seal, famously shared a speech and wrote a book, with his message that if you want to change the world, start by making your bed. This speech was so powerful and had such an impact on me, with the message that it's the little things in life that contribute to the big things. If you can't do the little things right, you won't do the big things right. Then, even if you try and fail at the tasks you're supposed to do that day or just have a miserable day, you will come home to a made bed and a feeling of accomplishment.

It is also important to embrace and be at peace with your inner child. The inner child is also noted as a source of strength, since early experiences can play a significant part in your development as an adult. This can go both ways – when childhood experiences negatively affect you, your inner child may continue to carry these wounds until you address the source.

Mental health is wealth. Each of us will need to heal ourselves mentally at some point. We are all different in how we deal with things. Asking for help is not a sign a weakness. It is important to talk, identify and acknowledge how we are feeling along the way.

Ways to heal yourself mentally:

- Value yourself. Treat yourself with kindness and respect, avoid self-criticism and self-loathing.

- Take care of your body. Taking care of yourself by eating healthy food and taking care of yourself physically can improve your mental health.

- Surround yourself with good and positive people – negativity can breed.

- Learn how to deal with stress. There are many methods to deal with stress, so find ones that work for you. Value laughter, research shows it can boost your immune system, ease pain, relax your body and reduce stress.

- Quiet your mind through meditation, prayer or relaxation methods.

- Set realistic goals. Decide what you want to achieve academically, professionally and personally. Aim high but be realistic, you will feel great self-worth and a sense of accomplishment as you work towards and achieve your goal.

- Talk and seek help when you need it. Seeking help is a strength, not a weakness.

- Find your happy place, pause and reflect when needed, get joy out of the small things.

Breaking down barriers
An aspiration of mine is to see a change in the world, to break down stereotypes and discrimination. We have come a long way but still have so far to go.

My children will have a different upbringing to what I did, but they will still be raised with the same core values of knowing that it's not money that brings opportunity and fulfilment, it's having good values, thinking outside of our bubble, questioning, pushing boundaries and making a positive impact on what we can change, with love and acceptance to diversity along the way.

I spoke about the pandemic being a new beginning and rebirth for me. I was in a bubble before. I thought I had to work hard to be as successful as I could be, resulting in making as much money as I could to provide for my family and enjoy the finer things in life, but that soon changed when March 2020 came.

Pausing in the pandemic was an eye-opener; it stripped things back to what really mattered. Helping people in need and paying it forward had just as much impact on me than changing someone's life through utilising my skills and professionalism in finding people new jobs.

I am so thankful I had the time to pause with my boys whilst they were young. Before the pandemic, my mindset was to work hard to provide them with the best life I could. When, actually, the best life for them is having me present and teaching them the value of kindness, acceptance and the importance of core values, to dream big and work hard to get there. Teaching them that life can be limitless and they can get so much satisfaction from helping others as well as chasing their dreams at the same time.

At We Recruit. Group our values are family comes first, honesty, transparency, paying it forward and being specialists in our field. We have identified our superpowers, utilised them in our business and encourage everyone on our team and in our networks to do the same.

I have held masterclasses on how to identify your superpower. Following three steps to identify yours and those around you is a game changer in life. I encourage the future generation to identify theirs early (I took mine for granted for so many years), and from doing this they can continue to develop and maximise success for themselves and their team.

In this age of digital distraction and living life through social media avatars and filters, it is important for us all to live with our eyes open so we can see the world around us. If we are not careful, we will fall into the trap of living in a digital world, missing out on the power of human connection, missing out on developing key relationships and human interaction which keeps our mind and soul young and happy.

Living our value of paying it forward is something I have instilled in my children for them to continue to practice in their lifetime. To pay it forward is an expression for when the recipient of an act of kindness does something kind for someone else, rather than simply accepting or repaying the original good deed.

Helping people where we could with the Virtual Coffee & Learn sessions and setting up WR Angels, volunteering our time and resources has been more impactful on me than winning any award in my career. The sense of purpose and how you can change something or someone is so powerful – sometimes we don't even know we do it, even a smile can go a long way.

The butterfly effect is mighty. Morgan Freeman quotes: 'How do we change the world? With one random act of kindness at a time.' Kindness costs nothing but has such a ripple effect. Teaching the future generation this from an early age will change the world.

An exercise we can all do to show kindness is to complete seven random acts of kindness in seven days:

- Day 1: Show your appreciation to someone in your life.

- Day 2: Show gratitude to a stranger.

- Day 3: Give a helping hand.

- Day 4: Listen.

- Day 5: Honour nature.

- Day 6: Make time to connect.

- Day 7: Pay it forward.

One of the main reasons I took the leap of faith and set up my own business was to have the flexibility needed with the demands of a young family. Times have changed that men are taking extended paternity leave and sharing the load, with many women returning to careers and the stigma of the stay-at-home mum being diminished. There is still a long way to go, supporting and pushing equality with our future generations and eliminating gender bias will help to promote and make equality a new norm to working parents, enabling people to maximise home and work life.

DANIELLE LOADER

Danielle is a global business owner with over twenty years of agency recruitment experience. An expert in her field, specialising in executive support recruitment, Danielle places executive assistants, chief of staff, business and office managers, alongside other business support professionals into their dream jobs and careers.

Danielle's mottos throughout her career and life have been 'changing lives' and 'always believe'.

Working across both the London and Australian market for over twenty years, she has experienced a variety of economic climates, with pivoting to change a key to her continued success.

As a mum of two young boys, experiencing toxic work cultures and witnessing burnout she understands the importance of putting her mental health first. In January 2020, Danielle took the leap of faith and became a co-owner of the now-global brand We Recruit. Group.

During the pandemic, Danielle built on her networks and offered support to those struggling to find work with monthly free 'Virtual Coffee & Learn' sessions. She also founded a volunteer group with like-minded women – WR Angels. Here they volunteered their time and resources to help charities and people in need to live their value – paying it forward.

Now CEO of We Recruit. Group Australia and with divisions in the UK and USA, as a group they continue to dream big and be limitless, with a focus on changing as many lives, through as many avenues, as possible along the way.

Website: werecruitgroup.com.au
LinkedIn: linkedin.com/in/danielleloader
Email: danielle@werecruitgroup.com.au

TOP TAKEAWAY TIPS

As first highlighted, life has definitely been a roller-coaster for me, as it will be for many of us. The important thing to remember along the way is the past is a story, it's the future that is unwritten. You can be limitless from tomorrow; how do you want to change tomorrow?

I am testament that if I can do it, anyone can, so dream big and take a leap of faith. In a world where you can be anything, be kind and always believe in yourself.

My tips to remember along the way are:

- Break down stereotypes. Don't conform to the norm; we can break down stereotypes one person at a time.

- Push through your boundaries. Life begins at the end of your comfort zone, so keep learning, take a leap of faith and dream big.

- Identify your superpower. This is our own particular genius, do not take it for granted. Once identified, build and maximise it, surround yourself with other superpowers, be limitless.

- Pay it forward. Know that kindness has a ripple effect in the universe – just smiling at someone in the street can make someone's day.

- Mental health is wealth. Be kind to yourself, pause and reflect when needed, practice self-care and understand the importance of balance.

BE ALL THAT YOU ARE TO BECOME ALL THAT YOU CAN BE

Emma Weaver

Sitting on my chair, looking at the rolling fields of green in front of me, my feet on the black cast iron bars that surround the veranda, taking it all in, I feel a sense of achievement and disbelief at how things have turned out.

You see, all of my dreams have come true. My vision is now my reality and I now understand there are no limits to creating the life I want, when it's done with heart and good intention. I come from a small village in Ireland, growing up in the countryside for many of the substantial years of my life. Becoming a mum at a very young age definitely spurred me down a different path than I thought was for me. You see, becoming a young mum in Ireland, traditionally means that's it, you're just a mum, unlikely to achieve anything more in life. Nothing comes after that.

So many of the generations of women that came before me it was accepted that any career was over as soon as they became pregnant, and the same was expected of me. I very easily could have fallen into that role – and very happily, I might add, because the unwavering love that I had for my daughter was enough to keep me fulfilled. However, I knew there was more to life. I had a feeling, a knowing, inside of me that there was more for me and I needed to show my daughter a different way, breaking the tradition of the generations of women who came before me.

One day, a health visitor came to see me and my little girl and we got talking; just a nice general chitchat of a conversation. She asked me what my aspirations had been before I unexpectedly got pregnant, and I explained that I always thought that I was going to finish school and go to university. I was going to be the one in the family to pave that path. I did finish school, however, I didn't do A levels or go on to university, all that had stopped when I became a mum. The health visitor, thank goodness, saw the passion in my face and knew that there was a spark in me. She had the vision to see what I could be and helped me enrol in my local college and further my education. That was the first step I took to change the way of those who had come before me. I put myself through college and graduated with my five-year-old daughter sitting on my knee. Honestly, it was unheard of at that time. It might sound like a small thing to a lot of people, but it was over twenty-six years ago now, and was an amazing achievement for a young mum, especially in rural Ireland.

It was a big thing in my eyes, and I needed plenty of discipline to achieve my goals and vision. It wasn't without its hardship. You see, to achieve things, sometimes you need to let go of other things. There's always a consequence to an action, either good or bad. There's always another side. So, we went without for several years to allow me to get through college. It all worked out well and my career started to take off.

Bringing my young daughter along with me as I progressed

through it, there were a lot of challenges, and a lot of things that I had to cope with – not least the death of her dad.

Along with the trauma, I was then a single parent, however, I did not dismiss my dreams. And it's strange, considering the environment that I grew up in, but I just knew, I had a feeling that there was more coming for me in my life.

So, working my way up through an organisation, I became the youngest manager to manage mental health services and continued to thrive for years in many different roles. My thirst for supporting and serving other people did not stop there. I'm the kind of person that, if I see a gap or a need in the community, will seek the resources to fill it. So, at that time, I set up an organisation across the north of Ireland for adults with ADHD, recognising that there was an ongoing need with little or no support for this particular group of people.

Who was I to do something like this? Who was I to think so big that I could create a charity that would support all of those adults who had no support? But I knew I could do it. I had the skill set required.

All my skills were transferable, you see. That's the beauty when you have vision and knowledge as well as experience behind you. Everything you learn in each experience is transferable to the next. That is what allows us to do different things, to find our purpose, do it passionately and share it with other people.

One of the most important things I've learned, that allows me to be limitless and to achieve all of these things, is to surround myself with the right people. And I don't just mean the cheerleaders, who say 'yes, you can do it. You're great, you're fabulous', I mean those people who are hard-hitting and will tell me cold, hard truths if they feel I'm doing a disservice or if I'm neglecting some aspect of my life – people to keep you grounded.

I sit here now as a successful entrepreneur of my company, Mental Wealth International, that is now global and achieving beyond my wildest dreams. Back when I started in mental health a few years ago, my dream was to serve people local to me to ensure that support went to businesses and community groups, in order to create cultures of wellbeing where I had recognised a growing need.

You see, the corporate world of mental health, the contracts and all the red tape, are not serving the people who need the support and services. You have to jump through so many hoops before you can even get support.

So, leaving my job after twenty-three years and going out on my own was courageous. I am a Leo, after all. Courage is certainly one of my strengths. My company became global at a very fast pace, although it didn't seem like it at the time. Five years after starting, it was almost unrecognisable in terms of how I was able to support companies, build teams and create cultures of wellbeing in all different areas of work – tech, construction, gyms, you name it. Mental Wealth International was sought after and recognised as a leader in its field. I had always had a global vision, but it was unimaginable what is now happening in my business.

The belief in what I was doing, who I was serving and the genuine desire to help others was so strong that it was recognised by many people. The big tech companies, big construction industries, gyms, all different organisations, were creating cultures of wellbeing, bringing in mental health and first aid learning through our interactive workshops, improving the lives of people tenfold. I never imagined the ripple effect that it was going to have. So, sitting here today is not about me. It's about recognising the collectiveness of the people that allowed me to break through my ceiling and support other people.

You see, once you begin to think limitlessly, you are able to create change for yourself and other people, paving the way for those coming after you. That's the thing about life, it takes many twists and turns along the way, and we need to learn from them. We need to share what we learn and pave the way forward. I quite easily could have fallen into the limiting beliefs that were bestowed on me as a young girl living in Ireland. And I could have sat back and accepted that there was nothing wrong with that. However, I knew there was more for me. I could feel it. I looked into the eyes of my daughter and wanted a different way for her. When you know your why, the how, what and when comes easily.

You need to believe, but more importantly, you need to take action. This all doesn't happen by chance. Take action, have a plan, create a vision. Bring others with you that truly believe in your vision and build from there.

Mental Wealth International went from strength to strength, because of my team who came along with me, sharing a vision that I could never have dreamed or imagined would be where it is today. It allowed me to create a life for myself and my family with choices and freedom, not only financially, but emotionally and mentally as well. I have the great privilege of leading a life by design, being able to step outside the nine-to-five grind that so many other people settle for.

And that is okay for them, when that is their vision. That is where they are. But there's one thing I know; you need to get out of your comfort zone if you want to achieve more. You need to get out of your own head. You need to take steps forward. Be courageous. Be curious about what goes on around you. Ask questions. Don't be afraid to be the only person in the room leaning forward with questions.

There are always options if you look close enough. The answer to everything lies within. I honestly believe the time that I spent building myself back up in my forties, learning who I was and who I was not, who I wanted to be and what I needed to do to get to that person, all helped me create my life. I enjoy being of service to others.

As I mentioned earlier, when I see a disservice, a gap or any amount of need, I feel compelled to find the resources to fill the gap. Surely as human beings, that is a beautiful way to be in life. So, build your dream, build your business, bring people with you and surround yourself with the right people. I'm not talking about the 'yes' people. I'm talking about the people who challenge you. When you do that, you will recognise that anything is possible.

Anything you desire is possible. You can make an impact. Do it with authenticity, as when you stay true to yourself, on the hard days, that is all you're going to be left with, regardless of who else you have in your life.

There have been many pivotal moments in my life: becoming a young mum, graduating, starting a national charity, leaving my secure job and building a business, collaborating with other people, creating opportunities for women through many different events and organisations. These pivotal moments have all led me here. And you can only join the dots backwards. Sitting here now, I'm taking it all in, understanding the resilience, the courage, the vision it took to get where I am today. I really feel that I have created an impact on the world, that I am leading the way for my children and their children, for better services for mental health and wellbeing across the world. It was something that started as a vision and I didn't know how it was going to happen, I just knew that it would.

So, think big, take action, be fearless and reach out. If you don't know the answer or you need support, we are all here to help you. And that is a beautiful thing.

You have the power within you
The realisation that I have the power within me to make things possible, regardless of what other people think, has happened.

Although feeling very afraid and needing reassurance and support from those around me who did think in limits, I knew I had something else within me. Though I didn't really know what, I knew there was something. So, getting myself back to college and graduating on 11 September, believe it or not, was one of those moments where I had my five-year-old daughter sitting on my knee and I knew I could do better things. I had what it took to dig deep, to get up on those dark mornings and get myself to college, leaving a crying baby behind, but knowing it needed to be done to get us to a better place, showing her that there is more to life when you've got something to give, and it's okay to do that.

So graduating was definitely one of those pivotal moments when I knew I had what it took to shake things up, to be different and think limitlessly. Another occasion was during the pandemic. Becoming unemployed, being made redundant in a job that I was in for over twenty-three years, I walked with my head held high and started my own business, creating a whole new world for myself and my family. But more importantly, bringing a positive influence to those impacted by mental health issues.

I began to create a new narrative around mental health, focusing on mental wellness and changing the way people think about it to be positive and inclusive. I believe we can achieve great things so long as we show up for ourselves and be consistent. So, while being a single mum with three children, I walked away from a secure job, where I'd worked for so many years, and set up my own business.

I was able to think bigger than others around me, and that can be a scary place to be in. You need to believe in yourself. You need to have an unwavering faith and vision, knowing you can achieve regardless of the obstacles. You are not who other people think you are. You are more than that. Take time out, as I do all the time, to sit in the silence and realise who you are and what you can achieve. Of course, there is fear, but you can turn that into your strength. Turn it into what fuels your passion and your ambition and you will, of course, achieve great things.

Whos limits are they?
When I've been faced with challenges or obstacles, I've often chosen to quietly write it down and embrace the feelings, while not letting fear or confusion override my thought process. I write down the pros and cons of what is happening and make my choices based on that. I use the outdoors, going for walks, for clarity through meditation.

Meditation allows me to trust in myself and the decisions I make in my life. I find it a very powerful tool. It's not very often that people tell me that I can't do something or I won't achieve something, knowing the kind of person I am and the determination I've shown throughout my life. However, there have been occasions when people have said, 'I'm not sure you can do that. It seems reckless what you're trying to do.' Especially when I accepted redundancy and walked away from a secure job, following my vision and passion for making impact with mental health in the world. But I recognise that was their limits. Their fear was coming from a place where they were at in their lives. When I took the redundancy, my teams did not want the change – they feared it. But everyone is replaceable and I know that. I was able to set aside all my emotions, all the feelings of attachment to my role and my colleagues; everything I'd achieved in the role. That awareness allowed me to recognise that I can succeed.

When I first spoke about my vision, I had expectations of family and friends, even acquaintances, to understand it, but now I realise, it's *my* vision, nobody else needs to 'get it'. So keeping myself in check, ensuring I have clarity on what I'm doing and a plan in place, I understand my way. Nobody can take that away from you, but you have to work on it, you have to write it down, you have to listen to yourself.

You need to find the strength on those hard days when others are doubting you, not to let that doubt spill into you. Follow your knowing and find your true self, otherwise it's not going to work. The voices of others will seep into your head. Be clear with your intentions of yourself, be honest with yourself, don't let fear overwhelm you. When you're honest with yourself and write down your true intentions, you can protect yourself from the doubting voices. How do I know this? Because I've been there myself. I feel, going forward, you need to go inside to understand yourself. You have a knowing of your how, your why, your what and your when. Knowing this, when others doubt you, will give you the strength to withstand their judgements, fears and adversity to change. When you are your true, authentic self and know your why, you will succeed in life.

Always reach back to those coming behind
For future generations, I feel it's important that we share our stories – our experiences in life, our wins, our losses, our successes

and failures, as well as what we learned from them. Be specific. Don't hold back. That way, people can understand and relate to you and your experiences. Be the lighthouse for those people who are trying to achieve great things and wanting to serve others.

We need to embrace them, show them the way and hold space for them in whatever way we can, by telling our story, not letting fear come between us. You can help others, sharing your successes with humility and an understanding of what it took to get there. Don't hide the loneliness, how hard it can be or how isolating it can be. That will allow others going through similar experiences to know they are not alone. This is what it takes to succeed.

Don't limit yourself. That could have very easily have happened to me, when I became a teenage mum. My world was very small. In fact, I could count the people in my life on one hand. So think big when it comes to your goals and dreams, no matter what others tell you. If others can do it, you can too. It's also important to recognise if you're on the right path and you're doing something because it's what you believe in. Quite often, our inspired thoughts or ideas come from a place where we have found a gap, or when we have been searching for something and it wasn't there.

Straightaway, you already know there is a need. However, there is also a need, of course, for whatever it is that you're trying to succeed in, whatever it is you're trying to change in the world and whoever it is you're trying to serve. You are unique in this world. Your take on it, your understanding, how you're bringing it forward, is unique to you. And there is room and space for whatever that may be.

The world needs it.

It's important to surround yourself with people who support you. I certainly could not have achieved the things I have alone.

And you don't have to either. With global technology these days, networking can be embraced worldwide, whether it's in person or online. Information is being shared and people are now showing up more authentically than ever. So surround yourself with the right people who allow you to think big. There are no limits except those that you put on yourself or allow others to put on you.

Embrace the new, be of service and grow
It's time to acknowledge that we must hold space for our future generations. We need to listen to them. We need to not try to keep them down or box them in. The world is a different place now than it was when I was younger, and we must embrace the change. Let's learn from our mistakes and not impose our beliefs on younger people. We need to recognise that the world is different, embrace the changes and all the good things that are in the world today. Technology is one of the biggest differences that is second nature to our young people. It takes patience and adversity to manoeuvre some of these new high-tech systems. Even some of the simpler things in life have changed. Our younger people have knowledge in things we don't understand. We need to listen to them to understand their values and where they are coming from. Of course, we can guide them. We can tell them of our mistakes, our failures and how we overcame them. We can show them how to be resilient. We need to not helicopter over them or make sure that everything is alright. Let's have real conversations about challenges, in our generations and theirs. Thankfully, there is an overlap. There are some things that are global and holistic, because at the end of the day, we are all human beings, and as human beings, we function the same. However, we don't all think the same. People's minds have developed in different ways. We know so much more about life, about what makes us think, about

our behaviours than we did even a few years ago. Or perhaps they did know more many years ago, but we just had no way to access that information the way we do now. We must step into the world that our future generations are looking and working towards and embrace their new thinking. What a breath of fresh air! It's amazing to listen to what they have to say.

A recent study conducted in over fifteen countries worldwide, found that globally, young people are more optimistic about the future than older generations. How amazing is that? This is even despite facing much higher unemployment rates, more instability and lower wages than us who came before them. The youth of today are entering adulthood confident that they can build a better future for themselves and those who follow. They are already thinking about future generations themselves. And I am not just talking about climate issues, I'm talking about lifestyle, what choices people are making and how it's going to look.

Things look very different now than they did even twenty years ago – however, some things remain the same. It is our duty to share our wisdoms without being judgemental. I do often say my parents gave me the wings to fly, but there was always a safety net below me, in case I should ever fall.

All of us should encourage our young people to try, and failure is part of that, and that's okay. We need to re-educate people or challenge people's thinking about what it is to fail – it is not the end result. There is always learning from it.

If you fail, don't take it personally. Stay on your path, strive for better things and surround yourself with those who can support you and help you to be intentional. Let's build better resilience, better role models, create change and work alongside our youth. From when I was very young, I was taught that adults always knew better and to respect your elders. I certainly agree with respecting our elders, however, our young people and our generations to come have a lot to say. Their words are of value. I want to be supporting our young people to stand up and speak their words. Let us embrace their perspective. Understand that nobody has to agree with *everything*. We just need to allow the space for young people to express themselves.

Surely in generations to come, the world will be a much different place, and we need to be ready for that. Let's work together as a collective alongside our youth and not assume that we know everything while trying to keep things the same. Change is inevitable. There's one thing we can all be sure of in this world, and that is that change happens.

Let's talk about what matters. What matters in the world now? What values do we need to keep? What things are working and what isn't? What is detrimental?

Can we encourage people to ask questions, be curious and think outside the box? There are no limits. Our young people are more adventurous now than ever. They have more platforms to express themselves and grow than we ever did. I come from an age where money certainly created divides, especially when wanting to have your voice heard.

Today, regardless of your status, there are so many mediums where you can be heard. So again, let's embrace it. Let's encourage everyone to speak freely, do good and be good, whatever that means in your world. Be curious, travel the world and learn about different cultures and different people. Dismiss judgements and stigma that is attached to so many things, because going forward in the world, we could do with less of that. There already is enough.

Speak to your friends about your vision. It doesn't have to be on a global stage. One person, five people, one hundred people. Create conversations about those things that matter. Dig deep, get meaningful. Find those people who support you, who understand what you're talking about. Create a plan. Hold your vision. Speak about it. Reach out. There is always someone who can help.

In the generation before us, where everything was siloed, people were so afraid that others would take their vision and idea and use it to become bigger themselves. But it doesn't work that way. Sharing allows you to have your voice heard. Let us not, as the older generations did, stagnate the growth of our youth. Let's embrace it. Let's do that safely, and make sure, as long as nobody is harmed, that your dreams can be realised. We are here for you. Let's be together as one.

EMMA WEAVER

Emma Weaver is the the founder of Mental Wealth International, an organisation supporting businesses to achieve better mental health and wellbeing within the workplace. Emma has over twenty-two years of experience working in the mental health and wellbeing sector.

Motivated by her purpose, Emma provides hope and expertise to people through both her personal and professional skills.

She is also an international bestselling author with her debut novel, *The Blue Line*.

As a two-time TEDx speaker she uses her voice to champion mental wealth.

Emma is *Passion Vista's* one to watch in 2021 and 2021 CIO women in business leader top 10.

THINK LIMITLESSLY

Email: emma@mentalwealthinternational.com
Website: www.mentalwealthinternational.com/
Linkedin: emmaweaver-mentalwealth
Instagram: @mentalwealthinternational & @emmaweaver01
Facebook: @mentalwealthinternational

TOP TAKEAWAY TIPS

- Find out who you are and stay true to your values as they are your constant and your compass.

- Surround yourself with the right people.

- Always take action when needed – be courageous in your mission.

- Recognise that you can have it all – you just don't have to do it all.

- Always be of service to others.

LIMITLESS: THINK GLOBAL

Hazel Herrington

Think Global is about my journey as a migrant woman from Zimbabwe to Australia and all the challenges and successes I encountered along the way.

I was born into a family of eight children in Zimbabwe. My parents had their hands full just trying to keep all of us fed and clothed, so there wasn't much room for investing in our education or sports careers. In high school, I excelled in a number of sports, including hockey, swimming and diving. I was even captain of the first team for many of these sports. But my parents could hardly ever attend our games due to their work and child care commitments, and they certainly didn't have the money to invest in our athletic endeavours. I felt like my parents didn't care, and it hurt me to see other parents supporting and encouraging their kids. What hurt the most was that I knew my parents loved me, but they just couldn't spare the time or money to invest in my athletic pursuits.

My family was ripped apart when I was sent to boarding school. I was 141km away from home, and I missed my family a lot. I cried every night because I wanted to go home. I eventually got used to boarding school, but it was hard for me to adjust. I missed my family a lot and felt really lonely. So sport became my release; it was something I could do to forget about my homesickness and focus on something positive.

I started to excel in swimming and diving, and eventually I was selected to travel to Kenya for a swimming and diving tour. This was a huge achievement for me, as it meant I could represent my country at international competitions. However, due to financial difficulties, my parents were unable to pay for my trip and I had to pull out.

I was so disappointed that I couldn't go, and I always wondered what could have been if my family had been able to support me. This experience made me realise that there were a lot of talented people out there who didn't have the same opportunities as I did, and this was something that I wanted to change.

I always wanted to share my love of sports with the world and knew that in order to do so, I needed to dream big. I couldn't limit myself or put any boundaries on what I could achieve. I had to believe in myself and know that anything was possible. When I chased my dreams and went for what I wanted, I was able to achieve some great things. And by sharing my passion for sports with others, I was able to bring happiness and joy to their lives too.

I began to understand that there was no limit to what I could achieve if I set my mind to it and worked hard. This realisation was empowering. It showed me that anything is possible if you're willing to put in the effort. As a woman, this was especially important for me as often we're told that we need to set lower expectations for ourselves than men. But through sport, I've been able to show that women can achieve anything we set our minds to. Sport has taught me a lot about being a leader and not quitting when the going gets tough.

In 2014, I decided to migrate to Australia. It was a huge decision, but I was determined to make a better life for myself and my family. My marriage was over, and I had to leave my two kids behind in Zimbabwe. It was one of the hardest things I've ever done, but I knew it was necessary in order to provide a better future for them. I cried every day for the first few months after I arrived in Australia. I missed my kids so much and worried about them constantly. But I was also motivated by the knowledge that I was giving them a better life.

I was ecstatic when I found out that I had been accepted to Griffith University. After working for many years and raising my children, I was finally able to go back to school and get my degree. It was a long journey, but it was worth it in the end. I am so proud of myself for completing my degree and becoming a successful businesswoman.

I am now the founder of Destiny Arise and I Am Bible Distribution Centre, two non-profit organisations in Zimbabwe that are committed to promoting women in leadership roles and equipping women and youth to become economically independent and wholly sufficient.

My goal is to create a more equal and inclusive world where everyone has the opportunity to excel in whatever they're passionate about. I want to help women and youth from disadvantaged backgrounds to reach their full potential. I believe that if we work together, we can make a difference and create a brighter future for everyone. So, dream big, think global and act local. Be the change you want to see in the world and never give up on your dreams.

Since arriving in Australia, I've continued to follow my dreams.

I started my own business and have been working hard to grow it. Now, as an entrepreneur, I'm using what I've learned from sport to empower other women and help them chase their dreams. I believe that every woman has the potential to be a leader in her own right. And through my work, I'm helping women all over the world realise their power and reach their full potential. Some of the skills I learnt from sport like teamwork, resilience and dedication are essential in business. I'm so grateful that sport has given me the opportunity to not only follow my dreams but to help others do the same. There is no greater feeling in life than knowing you've made a positive difference in someone else's.

So, whatever your dreams may be, don't let anyone tell you that you can't achieve them. Just because someone else doesn't believe in you, doesn't mean you should give up on yourself. Remember, anything is possible if you're willing to put in the hard work. And, when you do achieve your dreams, don't forget to pay it forward and help others achieve theirs too.

While there are many women entrepreneurs making a global impact, I believe it's important to also focus on women at the local level. This is because women are often the ones who are hardest hit by poverty and lack of opportunity. In many parts of the world, women are still not seen as equal to men. This means that they often don't have the same access to education, jobs or resources. As a result, women are more likely to live in poverty and be unable to provide for their families.

But when women are given the opportunity to thrive, they have the potential to change the world. When women are educated and empowered, they can lift their families and communities out of poverty. They can also serve as role models for future generations of women.

So, it's important that we continue to invest in women at the local level. This is how we will create lasting change and make a positive impact on the world. We need to remember that when we uplift women, we uplift entire communities. And when we give women the opportunity to succeed, everyone benefits. I'm living proof that anything is possible if you're willing to dream big and work hard. So, whatever your aspirations may be, never give up on yourself and always believe that you can achieve anything you set your mind to. Just like I did.

I'm a strong advocate for women's empowerment and I believe that sport can play a vital role in this. Sport gives women the opportunity to develop leadership skills and confidence. It is my vision to see more women in leadership positions all over the world, and I believe that sport can help make this happen.

As a woman trying to go global, I have faced many challenges and barriers. Here are some of the biggest challenges.

Lack of access to quality education and sporting facilities
It's no secret that when it comes to having access to quality education and sporting facilities, the wealthy often have a distinct advantage over those from poorer backgrounds. This was certainly the case for me when I was growing up. My parents couldn't afford to send me to a private school or pay for me to join a sports club, so I was stuck with the local state schools and clubs, which were often of a much lower quality than those available to wealthier children.

While it was certainly more challenging than if I had grown up in a wealthier family, I am proud of what I have achieved in spite of the obstacles that were put in my way. Access to quality education and sporting facilities should not be based on wealth; all children should be given the opportunity to achieve their dreams, regardless of their background.

Financial constraints

As I mentioned, my family wasn't wealthy, which meant that we often struggled to make ends meet. This had a major impact on my ability to participate in sport. Often, the only reason I was able to compete in tournaments and events was because my parents would scrimp and save in order to pay for my entry fees. And even then, we couldn't always afford the travel costs associated with getting to the event itself.

This meant that I often had to miss out on competitions that were taking place outside of our local area. And even when I did manage to compete, I was at a disadvantage because I didn't have access to the same resources as my wealthier peers. For example, I couldn't afford to attend a diving competition in Kenya.

Gender inequality

Unfortunately, gender inequality is still a major issue in many parts of the world, including Africa. This means that women often have to fight for their rights and opportunities, both in sport and in life more generally.

I was lucky enough to have parents who believed in my ability to succeed, regardless of my gender. However, not all women are so fortunate. In many parts of Africa, cultural norms and traditions mean that girls and young women are often not encouraged to participate in sport. And even when they are able to take part, they often don't have the same access to resources and opportunities as their male counterparts.

This needs to change. Women should be given the same opportunities as men, both in sport and in life. We need to work together to break down the barriers that are holding women back and create a level playing field for everyone.

Lack of role models

When I was younger, I didn't have any female role models in sport. This made it difficult for me to imagine myself as a successful athlete, because I had no-one to look up to or aspire to be like.

It is important for young girls and women to have female role models in sport, so that they can see what is possible if they set their minds to it. We need more women in leadership positions within the sporting world, so that we can inspire the next generation of female athletes.

The challenges of going global

Taking your sport to a global level is a huge challenge, no matter where you're from. But it's especially difficult when you're coming from a place like Africa, where there are often fewer resources and opportunities available.

For example, when I was trying to get my diving career off the ground, I had to self-fund my training and travel costs. This meant that I had to find creative ways to raise money, such as selling raffle tickets and holding bake sales. It was a lot of work, but it was worth it in the end.

If we want more African athletes to compete on the global stage, we need to provide them with the resources and support that they need. We need to invest in grassroots programs and create opportunities for young people to get involved in sport. And we need to break down the barriers that are preventing African athletes from reaching their full potential.

Sport has the power to change lives. It can give people the opportunity to achieve their dreams, regardless of their background or circumstances. However, there are still many barriers that prevent girls and young women from taking part in sport, especially in Africa.

We need to work together to break down these barriers and create a level playing field for everyone. We need to invest in grassroots programs and provide more opportunities for young people to get involved in sport. And we need to inspire the next generation of female athletes by increasing the visibility of women in leadership positions within the sporting world.

Only then will we be able to truly harness the power of sport to empower girls and young women all over the world.

Follow your dream
I was brought up believing that if you wanted something in life, you had to go out and get it. No-one was going to hand anything to me; if I wanted something, I had to work for it. And so, from a very young age, I started setting goals and working towards them. I was always a determined individual, but it wasn't until I was older that I realised the true power of following your dreams.

I started my career in leadership development and women's empowerment. I was working with different organisations, helping them to develop their people and achieve their goals. It was during this time that I started to realise my own potential. I began to see that there were no limits to what I could achieve; if I set my mind to something and worked hard enough, I could make it happen.

Lack of family support
One of the biggest challenges I faced as an entrepreneur was lack of family support. When I first started my business, my family didn't understand what I was doing or why I was doing it. They thought I was crazy to quit my well-paid job and try to start my own company. And so, for a long time, they didn't support me or my businesses.

It was only when they started to see the success of my businesses that they began to change their tune. They started to understand what I was doing and why I was doing it. And slowly but surely, they started to support me and my businesses.

However, even though my family now supports me, there are still times when lack of family support is a challenge. There have been times when I've needed help and advice from my family, but they haven't been able to give it to me because they don't really understand what I do. This can be frustrating, but I try to remember that they are supporting me in their own way and that's all that really matters.

Seeing my company grow and succeed was one of the proudest moments of my life. After I opened my first two businesses, I knew that I also wanted to empower other women to start their own business so that they could experience the same sense of achievement and fulfilment.

This is why I decided to launch my two charities Destiny Arise and I Am Bible Distribution Centre. These two non-profit organisations equip and empower women and youth to achieve their dreams and reach their full potential. We run financial literacy programs, business development training and we also provide seed funding and mentorship to help women get their businesses off the ground.

The work that we do is making a real difference in the lives of women and youth all over Africa. And I am so proud to be able to say that I am playing a small part in helping to create a brighter future for our continent.

However, there is still much more work to be done. There are still too many barriers preventing girls and young women from taking part in sport. And so, we need to continue working together to break down these barriers and create a level playing field for everyone. Only then will we be able to truly harness the power of sport to empower girls and young women all over the world.

My advice for anyone who is looking to achieve their dreams is simple: don't give up and don't let anyone tell you that you can't do it. If you want something badly enough, you will find a way to make it happen. So go out there and chase your dreams; they really are within your reach.

Think limitlessly
As a global leader, multi-award-winning entrepreneur, woman entrepreneur, global speaker and businesswoman, I believe that thinking limitlessly is key to success. It means always looking for new opportunities, pushing boundaries and taking risks. Global leaders who think limitlessly include Jeff Bezos, Elon Musk and Richard Branson. They are constantly innovating and coming up with new ideas.

Thinking limitlessly is also important for creating change. Mahatma Gandhi once said, 'Be the change you want to see in the world.' This is possible when we think outside the box and come up with new solutions to old problems. Finally, thinking limitlessly is essential for growth. As Thomas Edison said, 'There is no substitute for hard work.' By constantly challenging ourselves and expanding our horizons, we can achieve great things.

Overcoming challenges
When it comes to overcoming challenges, I always try to keep in mind what my goals are and why I am working towards them. It's very easy to get discouraged when people around you are not supportive of your choices, but if you can keep your focus on what you want to achieve, then that will help you push through any obstacles. In terms of dealing with different expectations, I

usually try to communicate with the people involved and explain why my choices are important to me. It can be difficult to balance all of the different demands on your time and energy, but by staying focused on your goals and keeping a positive attitude, you can make it through anything.

I am a woman entrepreneur and global leader. I juggle the expectations of family and friends, work colleagues and my vision. I am constantly thinking global and innovating to change the world. I face challenges every day, but I know that my strength comes from God. I am determined to succeed in everything I do. My family and friends are my support system, and they help me to stay focused on my goals. My work colleagues are a great source of support, but they can also be a distraction. I have to stay focused on my vision and not let anything or anyone get in the way of my dreams.

Think big

Many young people are told not to think big. They are often given small goals to achieve, and many times these goals are not their own. Society tells them what they should do, instead of letting them figure out what they want for themselves. This can be frustrating for young people who have dreams and aspirations that are much bigger than what is expected of them.

However, there are things that young people can do to increase their chances of achieving their goals and living the life they want. The first is to stay positive and never give up on their dreams. No matter what others say, it is important for young people to believe in themselves and their ability to succeed. They also need to be willing to work hard and make sacrifices in order to achieve their goals.

Finally, it is important for young people to surround themselves with positive people who will support them in their quest for success. These individuals can provide encouragement and guidance when needed and can help keep them focused on their goals. With these things in mind, young people can achieve anything they set their mind to.

How our future generation can contribute

Unity and peace

I would love to see the world become a more peaceful place. I think our future generation has the potential to make a real difference in this area. They can do this by reaching out to others and spreading messages of peace and unity. I also hope that our future generation will be more environmentally conscious. We need to take steps now to protect our planet, and I believe the next generation will be up for the challenge.

Being more environmentally conscious

The environment is something that I am very passionate about. We need to be more conscious of the impact we are having on the planet and take steps to reduce our carbon footprints. I think young people can really make a difference in this area, and I hope they will choose to do so.

Poverty alleviation

I would also love to see our future generation make a difference in the area of poverty alleviation. There are so many people around the world who are living in poverty, and I think we have a responsibility to help them. I believe that our future generation has the potential to make a real difference in this area. They can do this by working to raise awareness of the issue and helping to fundraise for organisations that are working to combat poverty.

Accepting different cultures and religions

With the world becoming more and more connected, it is important that we learn to respect and appreciate the differences between us. I believe that our future generation has the potential to make a real difference in this area by being open-minded and promoting understanding and tolerance.

Standing up for social justice

There are so many issues in the world that need to be addressed, and I believe young people have the power to make a real difference. They can do this by speaking out against injustice and by working to promote equality. In Africa, women entrepreneurs are playing a big role in standing up for social justice and equality. I believe that our future generation can learn from their example and make a difference in the world.

Promoting gender equality

I believe that women should have the same rights and opportunities as men. Our future generation can make a real difference in this area by working to promote gender equality in all areas of life. As a migrant woman I have experienced firsthand the importance of gender equality because it is only when women are on an equal footing with men that we can truly progress as a society. The SDG goals offer a great framework for promoting gender equality and I hope our future generation will take advantage of them.

Encouraging economic development

Our future generation can make a real difference in the area of economic development by working to promote entrepreneurship and fostering innovation. I think young people have a lot to offer in terms of economic development, and I believe they will play a big role in shaping the future of the world economy. We can encourage economic development in Africa by supporting women entrepreneurs. They are playing a big role in boosting the economy and creating jobs.

Advocating for human rights

Human rights is another issue that I am very passionate about. I believe that everyone deserves to be treated with dignity and respect. Our future generation can make a real difference in this area by working to promote human rights in all areas of life. In Africa, women entrepreneurs are playing a big role in advocating for human rights. I believe that our future generation can learn from their example and make a difference in the world.

Global leadership

Our future generation has the potential to be leaders in the global community by working to promote understanding and cooperation between different cultures. We can encourage global leadership by supporting women entrepreneurs.

Work ethic

Finally, I believe that our future generation can make a difference in the world by setting an example with their work ethic. They can do this by working hard and being creative and innovative in their approach to work. We can encourage a strong work ethic by supporting women entrepreneurs.

As you can see, there are many things I would love to see happen in the world. These are just a few of my hopes for our future generation. I believe that if we work together, we can make all of these things a reality.

HAZEL HERRINGTON

Hazel Herrington is a successful entrepreneur, marketing and branding expert, CEO and founder of Herrington Publications Worldwide and dedicated to empowering entrepreneurs to become economically independent and wholly sufficient worldwide.

Hazel has won multiple awards for her work in entrepreneurship and empowering women, including the 2022 Entrepreneurship Award at the National Migrant Achiever awards in Australia, the World Greatness Award by Greatness University in the United Kingdom and nomination for the Australia Top 100 Women of Influence Award.

Through Herrington Publications Worldwide, Hazel publishes books and magazines that empower women through personal development programs and courses, and she also leads business conferences, workshops and webinars.

HAZEL HERRINGTON

Website: herringtonpublications.com
Email: info@herringtonpublications.com
Phone: +61452520841
LinkedIn: dr-hazel-herrington
Instagram: @herringtonpublications & @hazelherrington_publisher
Facebook: @HerringtonPublicationsWorldwide
Twitter: @HPWTWEET

TOP TAKEAWAY TIPS

- Be passionate about something. We are all more likely to make a difference in the world if we are passionate about something.

- Be informed. Make sure you are well-informed about the issues you care about. This will help you to have a better understanding of the problems and how you can contribute to solving them.

- Be creative. Think outside the box and come up with new and innovative ways to make a difference.

- Be persistent. Don't give up, even when things get tough. Remember that every little bit counts and eventually your efforts will make a difference.

- Be positive. Stay positive and believe in yourself and your ability to make a difference. This positivity will inspire others and help you to achieve your goals.

I hope these tips have inspired you to make a difference in the world. Remember, we all have the power to change the world, one person at a time. So, let's get out there and make a difference!

AWAKEN YOUR POTENTIAL

Karen McDermott

I'm going to share with you a little masterclass that I do when I work with people who haven't awakened to their potential. The reason I'm so passionate about helping people awaken to their full potential is because I know that anything is possible. There is nothing you can't achieve when you set your mind to it. If you want it, you can have it.

No excuses

It's easy to make excuses not to achieve something, but the fact is, you can achieve anything if you want it. You set an intention, you take inspired action and you follow through. You have to have the courage. Invest in yourself, whether that be through time or money, and when you connect with the right people, you can feel very in-tune with what it is you want to achieve.

You really can achieve anything in your life. I stand here at forty-five years old in 2022, having achieved more than many people do in ten lifetimes. And why is that? It's because I don't have limits to what I believe is possible. I know I can achieve anything when I set my mind to it.

I have the courage to pursue all of my dreams and desires and to action things that need to be actioned. I'm also very strategic. I'm very connected to my ability to know what is the next best step on my journey to receiving. One of the things I bring it back to is self-awareness. We need to do the work on ourselves, to become aware of our abilities and where our strengths lie. When we understand ourselves, we can better assess what is required to achieve our desires.

And we need to increase our awareness when we want to achieve big things.

Most important is getting clarity on what it is you really want. Many people don't know what they want. They get confused, or they want too many things. They think they want something, when in actual fact, they don't, because it's not aligned with their higher purpose.

Take a moment, now, to identify with your values and really consider if what you think you want is aligned with them. It's so important not to compromise any of yourself in the process of receiving. This is a huge mistake I see many, many people make when they want to manifest or achieve things they believe are impossible.

Allign with your values

So, know your values, have self-awareness and know what matters to you, because honestly, if you want to go for something and you achieve it, you don't want to have sacrificed any of your values on the journey.

An example of this is that I'm a mum of six. I love being a mum, but I also love achieving things. I have a limitless belief system, so I can make anything happen, but what if something I want compromises my values? Is it worth it? If it means I'm not available for my children, for me that's a 'hell no'.

So when I am knowing and setting intentions in the pursuit of my goals, I always make sure I truly understand what I want and connect with it. That's what it's going to take to make something happen. I ask myself, *Is it aligned with my values and is it worth it?* Because I can guarantee you, by the time you get to the destination of receiving that goal, if you have to compromise your values to get there, it will not be worth it.

No monetary or personal goal is worth compromising your values, whether that be your family or a part of yourself. You've got to consider what will be detracted from your life to make your goal happen.

If you're able to truly identify what it is you want, and what you want to make happen is aligned with your values, you can also see what good you can do for others on your journey. It's always good to give. There are some amazing businesses and organisations in the world that give up to 10% of all their earnings to charity. Some people just know that by giving part of what they receive to others, so much gratitude is being poured into them, which in turn, will create a circle of abundance.

Step-by-step process
So, if you cannot see too far ahead or if things get overwhelming for you when you think of limitless beliefs, then take it step by step. Set the goal but then just go on the journey and take it one step at a time until you get there. I set myself the intention of building a million-dollar publishing press. I thought it would take me twenty-five years, but I dedicated myself to the journey. I was open to opportunities and I'm very aware and in-tune with my

knowing. It only took seven years to achieve my goal, a third of what I originally thought.

So, how do you do that? Just be open, aware and have the courage to take action when it's needed.

Think about it.

- Set an intention

- Follow it by actioning inspired thoughts and/or opportunities (understand that they are going to come in unconventional ways, because you can't change things if you're doing it in the same way you've always done it).

- Action it! This takes courage, but remember that taking the same actions will get you the same results, so in order to achieve things, you've got to think differently. You've got to action different things and have the courage to do that.

Magic happens outside your comfort zone

That, of course, is outside of our comfort zones. We're humans. But I can tell you, 100%, that the magic happens just one step outside your comfort zone. And if you have the courage to step outside of that every time you take an action, guess what you're going to be doing? You're going to be reaching limits that you never dreamed possible before.

You're going to surpass any ceiling you ever had. And when you get there, you discover that's not the end of it, you have more to come! Have you ever set a goal or intention that you surpassed tenfold? Because sometimes, when we set the intention to achieve something, it's where we're at right there in our minds, in that moment. It's hard for us to see further, because it's beyond us.

By being a limitless believer, you know that there's no ceiling on what can be achieved, so it may look very different than what you imagined.

Believe in yourself
When we believe in ourselves, we can make the most amazing things happen.

Believing in ourselves is one of the biggest and most important things we can gift ourselves. If you don't believe in yourself in the first instance, lean on someone and allow them to believe in you and be energised by that. Because when people believe in you it can be very motivating. And you can take action from that.

If I hadn't believed in myself when I started out on my journey, I certainly wouldn't be where I am today. And it was because someone believed in me and my work that I began to believe in myself.

If no-one is believing in you, then you're hanging out in the wrong circles. You've got to surround yourself with people who lift you up. All the people who want to lift you up believe in you, so use that as evidence to believe in yourself.

So, think limitlessly. Leave room for the magic and don't be afraid to share the journey, the trials and tribulations, the triumphs. There are so many people sharing their journey right now, but it's mostly about their vulnerabilities, which is wonderful because they have other people with them on the journey. However, where are the people sharing their triumphs and their success stories? I believe we need more of that right now, as you can't just achieve something and keep it to yourself.

That's not the way the world is supposed to work. We're supposed to learn how to do something and share those skills with other people. I'm often asked, 'Karen, how do you do it?' It can seem totally illogical to some people for a mother of six to achieve everything I've achieved. And yet I don't overthink it.

Smell the roses
I will someday sit and write my life story, from day to day, about how I got to where I am. But right now, I'm forward focused. I don't reside in the past, I am supercharged in the present. And that ensures that my future is always bright. This is only possible for me because I have the courage and the belief in myself that anything is possible, should I choose to achieve it.

But I do always make sure it's aligned with my values.

Being future focused with my limitless thinking means, for me, that I build upon the foundations for both authorship and publishing that I have set in stone. I have also set my foundations for motherhood, because I do want it all. I want to be a really good mum, present for my children no matter what age they are. And I also want to have an impact with my writing.

I know that my writing and my universal thinking is an inspiration for others, so I've shown up and I've written a lot of books on the subject. I'm building up my YouTube channel that will be a resource for people who are awakening to their true potential through publishing. My publishing houses are amazing and they are not overly systemised, so I still have to be present on the journey. But the publishing happens really well, and it's not so time-consuming for me, as the logistics rely on my amazing team. We are future focused in getting books out there, further and wider, in different languages and to make amazing things happen for our authors.

That's where my publishing houses are unique. It's one thing for an author to write a story, going on that publishing journey and leveraging it to build a brand, but we want more people to read our stories, because our authors' words are making a difference and have a positive impact on the lives of others. We have put together a really good bookstore, with added elements of online book clubs, affiliation agreements, charitable incentives and a wonderful energy around being that resource for buying.

Always keep moving forward
I'm so excited about the future for what I can do limitlessly. It's funny because ten years ago I would never have thought I would be where I am today. I could never have foreseen it. I could never have set the intention for it because I have surpassed what my mind could have envisioned for myself.

My advice to anybody reading this chapter is to be open to the journey.

Let go of control
Don't try to control everything, keep your eyes on the periphery of your vision. Be very connected to your power of knowing when making decisions, so that you make decisions with unwavering confidence. Make decisions for your next 'best' step and understand the power that a 'no' can bring. Because if your heart is not in it, you're doing a disservice to the person you say yes to, and also to yourself. You're wasting your time and their time; time that can be given to what you are building and what your heart and your purpose is focused on.

So, know that you can have it all without having to compromise your values. It's so much more pleasurable when you enjoy the journey and don't focus too hard on the destination. Be open and embrace opportunities, and you'll be surprised at what comes your way, because it could never have been predicted. And when I live through this, I have huge success. It is very much an energetic thing for me, as much as it is a mindset.

When you combine both masculine and feminine together, you have a magical combination. A success formula that is forever growing and achieving is one that is so fulfilling because you don't have to compromise any of yourself in the process. In fact, time just whizzes by because you're doing what you love, everything you need for the next step comes to you and the journey doesn't end. And you don't want it to end because what you're doing is igniting your soul, it's filling your cup, it's helping you give the best of you to others. Isn't that magical?

As much as this is a business book, it's also where business meets our intuitive abilities. Intuition is something we all have. We all have the ability to know. We all have the ability to make a difference for ourselves, and in turn that makes a difference for others. It's when we're making a difference for ourselves that we show up as the best version of ourselves. One of the things I really want people to understand about limitless beliefs is that we have to put ourselves first before we can give to others.

It's not about sacrificing everything you have so that somebody else can have it, or so that we can help someone else. All of the world's greatest people, all amazing givers, knew how to give to themselves first. Then they had so much more to give others. Do the math.

It's everything together; maths and science, quantum physics, energy. If you are energised, you have so much more to give. So remember, for those people who give a lot, please make sure you remain energised and know how wonderful it is for you to do that. You can't afford to burnout, because if you do, you're going to be no good for anyone. It's not selfish to put yourself first so you can live limitlessly, as this inspires others and helps amazing things happen for them along the way.

KAREN MC DERMOTT

Karen is an award-winning publisher, author, TEDx speaker and advanced law of attraction practitioner.

Author of numerous books across many genres – fiction, motivational, children's and journals – she chooses to lead the way in her authorship generously sharing her philosophies through her writing.

Karen is also a sought-after speaker who shares her knowledge and wisdom on building publishing empires, establishing yourself as a successful author-publisher and book writing.

Having built a highly successful publishing business from scratch, signing major authors, writing over thirty books herself and establishing her own credible brand in the market, Karen has developed strategies and techniques based on tapping into the power of knowing to create your dreams.

Karen is a gifted teacher who inspires others to make magic happen in their lives through her seven life principles that have been integral in her success.

Website: serenitypress.org & kmdbooks.com & mmhpress.com

TOP TAKEAWAY TIPS

- Believe that there are no limits on what you can achieve and your results will be more than you can imagine.

- See the unseen opportunities by opening your mind to peripheral thinking.

- Take time to get clear on what it is you want to achieve.

- Love life and it will love you back.

- Run your own race! Stay in your own lane. And set your own goals.

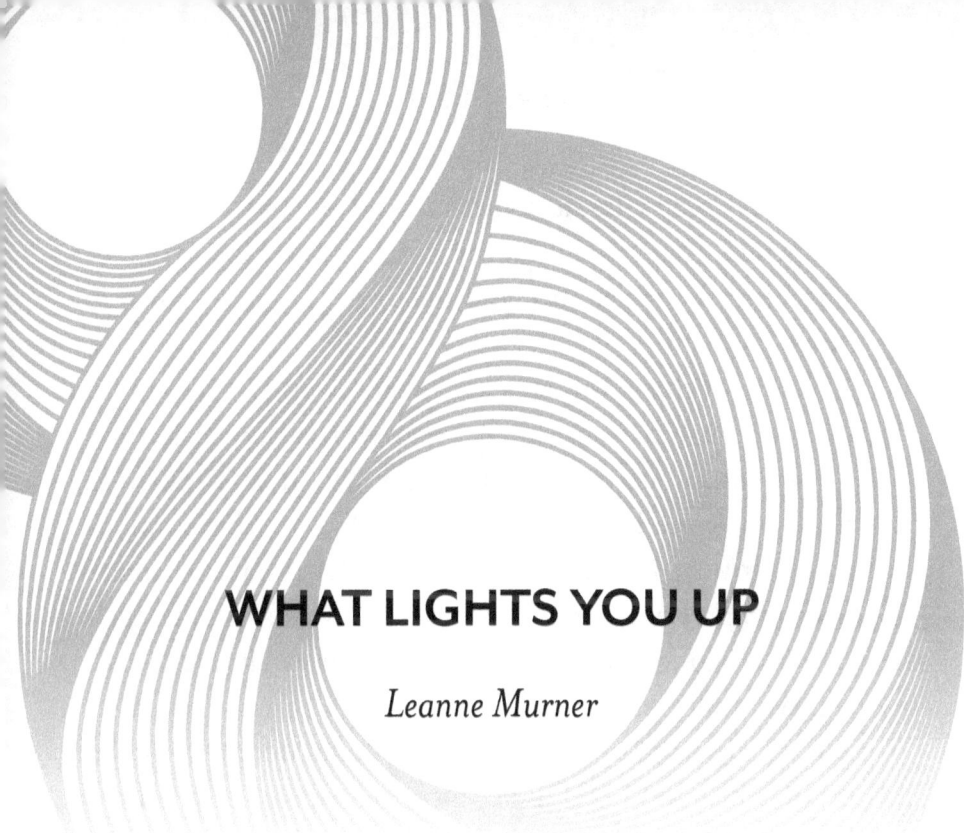

WHAT LIGHTS YOU UP

Leanne Murner

Stopping at nothing

I was a headstrong child with so much drive and determination; no matter what dream or desire I had, I chased it. My ideas were crazy at times but that's what lit me up. I wasn't one to be out with friends on the weekend – I spent a lot of my spare time doing woodwork and craft and then sold it at a local market; I loved being creative. I worked three part-time jobs all before I was seventeen. I was saving for my first home, which I purchased at twenty, and ticked off one of my childhood life goals. I had always said why pay off someone else's mortgage by renting when I can pay off my own home. I didn't have the support I thought I would get from friends and family and was told I was just showing off and trying to be someone I wasn't.

This was a goal I had set so many years earlier and to finally achieve this showed me that thinking limitlessly was the way to make dreams come true no matter the adversities you're faced with. This milestone helped set my mindset that I could achieve anything I put my focus into, and this brought me so much joy and excitement.

This state of mind was quickly taken away as I fell into an abusive relationship. Everything I had worked towards for so many years was gone in the blink of an eye. It was something that really took me by surprise; I just didn't see this coming. I had gotten myself into a situation that I felt I had no control over. Everything I had been focusing my life on since the age of fifteen was all gone – it was like the rug was swept from under my feet. My milestone, the one thing I was so committed and focused on achieving to show me that I could do anything, had also become his, and I had to accept this mistake I had made so that I could allow myself to be free and move on with my life. Starting fresh and finding a new journey was the only way I knew I could rebuild. I had done it once; I could do it again.

Initially, I withdrew for several months, trying to process what had happened and where my path was leading me. I needed to get out of the house. I needed to push through my grief, my loss and my shock and overcome this hurdle so that I could move forward with my life. I was turning into a person that was losing hope and motivation, and this was not the real me. I needed to tap into my inner self-knowing that I was so much more than where I then stood. The real me was still inside and I was going to be okay. I knew there was a new journey that was waiting for me.

'The world as we have created it is a process of our thinking. It cannot be changed without changing our thinking.' – Albert Einstein

I bought a camera and started to take landscape photographs. As someone who has always been creative, taking photographs ignited me and rekindled those feelings I had when I was younger, it got me thinking that I could make a business from this very thing that I loved – taking photographs. So, some months later, I found myself back at the markets selling my landscape photos, turning a hobby into a business which then expanded into family portraits, newborn shoots and later weddings. At this stage, I had just had my first child and realised I did not want to go back to full-time work, and it was at this stage my next business venture began.

As a small photographer, I couldn't afford bulk photography packaging. But as I canvased other local photographers, I soon realised that they too were in the same boat. Looking back, I was quite innovative, as I then decided to take a leap and purchase bulk. I started to sell on to local photographers, solving the dilemma we were all experiencing. This quickly expanded to selling international. Being the only business having no minimums to order, we expanded very quickly, purchasing printers and engravers and offering a custom service with personalised products with clients' names and logos. This growth was exponential as we quickly grew to five staff, and my husband needed to also come onboard.

This growth phase occurred over the next four years as we expanded our family with an additional four children. Looking back, it was no easy task, and most would say it was impossible, but when you love what you do and you do it with those that you love, it all becomes easy. I chose to stay home to care for my family as well as run a successful business, one that was able to sustain with the growth of a family with five children.

However, five years later, I realised that the love I once had for this work was no longer fulfilling me. Having children changed my perspective in life and in what I wanted for them, just as much as what I wanted for myself. That lens of a parent takes you into their future, and I began to see plastic toys and games consuming my house, and this is where I realised I could do something different. I began to create and manufacture wooden products for children. I tested the market by offering some of the timber offcuts to my local preschool for arts and craft play, but as I shared this with the staff, they suggested I could do something better – puzzles. This was exactly what I needed – once again that creativity was ignited in me. I started to research and noticed there wasn't any Australian-themed puzzles on the market; kids knew what an elephant and lion was but not a wombat or a Tasmanian devil, so I used the scrap wood to create puzzles and games and started to sell them to schools and early childhood centres. This quickly escalated and placed our Australian products on an international platform. Little did I know, but as this business grew, it began to also influence my boys. Every time I made a new product, I would bring it home for them to test and give their feedback. I started to research animals, plants, ecosystems and started to discover the state the world was in. When looking back, I realise how grateful I have been that the thing that brought me joy and creativity at work also included my boys as they shared this journey with me, learning along the way as they helped to creating the timber products.

The more I learnt, the more I realised that the information I was absorbing was more than what was going into the puzzles and games. There was information in these products that sparked an interest for the children. They were really engaged and wanted more.

Some months later someone suggested I put what I knew it into children's books, and I laughed, saying, 'I barely got through school, how am I going to write children's books?' This suggestion was out of my comfort zone, and yet, as I sat back to reflect on my response, I realised that not only was it possible, I also wanted to show my boys that when you put your mind to something, everything is possible, just like me buying my first home at the age of twenty. I have since learnt that you can't grow by staying in your comfort zone. What I should have been saying to myself was, *Who am I* not *to write a children's books?*

As an adult, I have struggled with getting out of my comfort zone. I was fine taking risks, but when it came to having the spotlight placed on me, I was straight back into my shell, playing small, and I hated being the centre of attention. I was not used to it, and I soon realised that this had also had a huge impact on me expanding in my previous businesses (despite me being recognised with awards and being interviewed with published articles, I somehow played small). What I have come to realise is that you do not grow staying in your comfort zone and you can't expand by staying in your shell.

My whole life I have felt I was always chasing acceptance for what I was doing and wanted to fit in, I wanted to have that family who was proud of me and showed support for achieving my dreams, to have some close friends that encouraged all my crazy ideas and showed their support, but I was that square peg fitting in that round hole – I even had a friend ask me how I could run a business and not even have a degree. This statement sat with me for a long time and made me question every thought and idea I ever had.

It is interesting that society tells us that having a degree enables us to accomplish different things, but doing it somehow is not enough! On reflection, I realised that undertaking a degree was not going to light me up, but being prepared to think different, be creative and push through barriers would. That childhood drive and determination is what brings about change, and that is what I now rely on.

Throughout my life I never wanted to follow in someone else's footsteps, I wanted to create a life so that one day someone wanted to walk mine. When we limit our thinking, we limit our life and opportunities that may follow.

As a kid I was always taught that if you needed help you were weak, and don't you dare ever think you were worthy enough for praise. Weak people need help and seek praise, so I never thought I deserved either. Now, being a global award-winning author and having the journey I have been on, I have experienced so much growth within myself, overcome so many obstacles and couldn't have done it without the help and support of my amazing friends and family.

'If you want to have a breakthrough in your life, you have to break your patterns.' – Dr Nicole LePera

This is where I started my journey as an author; the inspiration I was receiving from my boys and including them on this journey was creating questions that I couldn't answer. I have now realised that I have found my calling and my chance to create impact. Most importantly, I was open to help to achieve this milestone.

Now, after publishing my first seven books, I have learnt the importance of education within the younger generation. I can see through what my boys are learning as they join me on this journey , they now know how important our ecosystems and wildlife really are. All my published work is creating awareness around native plants, what they need and who needs them to survive. All my research has been a real eye-opener on so many levels, from the habitat loss and extinction of our wildlife, to pollution of our waterways and oceans, chemicals on our foods and soil and in the air we breathe. This is not something that can be shrugged off and put into the too-hard basket, it's real-life and all this is happening around us – and not just in Australia, but globally!

Having a story creating so much awareness around these topics needs so much content and I am finding it is just too much for a children's book. This is where thinking limitless has come into play again for me. I have created a team to help expand this into educational packs for schools, early childhood, homeschooling and parents wanting to explore these topics with their children. This way my stories can be told with the overflow of information extended in these activities and worksheets. Furthering the education to our children about the state of the planet is critical in today's day and age. If we don't start to create awareness around these topics there may not be a world for these children and their children which is quite scary. Reality is 'you don't know what you don't know', but sparking this awareness in our children creates conversations with family and friends creating a flow-on effect into the current population.

It's okay to be different
I think, as humans, we believe that we are expected to conform to what everyone is doing rather than to what is aligning for us as individuals. This can result in missing signs of new possibilities. Being that square peg wanting to fit into a round hole made me different, but I have since discovered I was never meant to fit in. I am here to make a difference, and that requires me to be different and think limitlessly. Looking at life, we are all so conditioned into a world of everyone thinking we should all want the same things (just so we do not feel left out). This being the case, the world is filled with everyone thinking and doing the same thing with a fear of being different or judged.

That's no fun – you need to be the real you, go against the grain, this is where we discover our real power, our power within.

I unleashed this power in becoming an author. The first time I held my first book was the most rewarding time for me; to physically hold it in my hands, knowing I wrote it, I felt like a part of me just ignited inside, and I just wanted more. It took me back to when I was in primary school, I was at the bottom of my class, repeated grade five and just didn't feel connected to anything educational whatsoever! Wow, how things can change with timing and the belief you have in yourself. Having now published seven children's books in the space of eighteen months has confirmed that stepping out of your comfort zone and accepting help when needed has gotten me to this point, but now I am wanting more. This achievement has sparked a need to do more and create impact in educating the next generation through stories and resources. This is now where my passion lies, I have found what lights me up. With the support of my boys, I now know what my reality is.

Taking time out
I have learnt so much as I have navigated through my journey, from disappointment of being let down, to absolute elation of winning a global award for my very first book. Life will always give you ups and downs, but it's the power you hold within you that enables you to strive for more.

When I was getting ready to launch my seventh book, I was burnt-out. I had worked so hard to get myself to this point I just couldn't continue. I started to second-guess everything I had done; I was slowly unravelling the path I had just taken, and everything was all happening so quickly I was not mentally ready for it. I pushed myself so hard to get everything processed so quickly I started to question myself. Was this the journey I was meant to take?

I was excited for where I was heading but struggled with being rewarded for everything I was doing. I had won five awards, one being gold for author of the year. I had never won anything except the occasional meat tray at the local club raffle prior to that. Receiving these awards placed me in a state of shock – I was frozen and very emotional. This had meant so much to me, but somehow, I wasn't able to process it all. I had come so far but had no idea what to say. I was the centre of attention, but I had not anticipated winning so there was no speech prepared. I remember rambling whilst drying my tears and then just ended things abruptly. These wins were confronting and took a toll on me, so much so that I needed to take six months off to process, reflect and begin to plan a road map forward.

Taking time out was the one thing that allowed me to reflect with clarity, and the thing I love most is camping with my family. We took time out in a lush green forest for two weeks with no phone service and no outside world to distract me. This was a recharge – a place where we got back to nature and felt grounded once more.

I really connected with myself and started to think about what it was I really wanted and how I was going to get there. It was in this moment, down by the water's edge as I lay on my paddleboard watching the clouds go by, that my mind was still. I had no other thoughts or distractions and felt like I was at peace.

As you might imagine, being a mum to five boys, I don't get much quiet time.

As I lay there, looking out onto the water, I noticed a blue butterfly flying around me and then suddenly it landed on me, almost like it wanted to share a secret. At first, I was startled and then my heart raced.

I have a freaking butterfly on me! I put my hand out in front of it and it crawled onto my hand. There was this incredible connection. This delicate and special insect was sitting there connecting with me.

I sat there observing how intricate this little creature was, I had not realised that I had spent nearly half an hour with it on me. It was the most amazing thing I had experienced, just being in the moment.

This was a sign from the universe, to get my attention to just stop and observe. Be at ease and at peace with myself.

The next morning, I went for an early walk and sat by the river writing in my journal. I started to express how I was feeling, it had been some time since I was able to feel any peace, but yesterday that time with the butterfly allowed me to realise that there was more for me, if I allowed it. In that moment I felt like there was a shift in my perspective. I was calm, and as I realised that, I was again graced by my beautiful blue butterfly.

What are the chances of having a blue butterfly come and visit you twice in the space of two days! I looked at it as if it could understand me and said, 'Okay, you have my attention; I am listening!' as if I would hear its response. The truth is that in that moment whilst I was asking it for guidance, I was discovering it from within.

Now some of you may not believe in these random acts, but for me, I have learnt to pause and be aware of everything around me. So being conscious of my experiences with the butterfly, I took the opportunity to look at the spiritual meaning of a butterfly. This allowed me once again to pause, breathe and to cry. It's meaning is 'transformation'. This was my inner self, allowing my conscious self to step forward to be the person I now choose to be.

Having this time out in nature was exactly what I needed to focus on the path ahead. I now know that I want to create a greater impact in the world through my books, and to do this I needed to stop, pause and focus on the way ahead. It was at this time that I also had an amazing friend stand by me, encouraging me that the road forward was there for me, when I was ready. Her support enabled me to see my strengths again, and with this newly regained insight, I now know that my lessons and experiences have all been part of journey, so that I can become the person that I am today.

Thinking out of the box
I struggled when I first started with the education puzzles. I wanted children not only to learn from what I was creating but to also stay engaged enough to want to learn more. But the more I researched, the more I realised that I would enhance these learnings through books and stories. Since writing these books, my whole vision has changed, and this has now allowed me to look at other possibilities which excites me as the opportunities are really endless.

With climate changes happening all around I have put my focus into creating stories that will educate and encourage the younger generation to want to make a difference for their future. This now has encouraged me to seek out like-minded people to collaborate with so that we can create a greater impact. I have now also been able to reflect on my previous businesses and my inability to step out without it having an impact on my business. The importance of collaboration, having a team, being able to share ideas and rely on one another has now become a reality for me and something I will now explore so that we can collectively move forward.

Having goals is one thing but to implement them is another; feeling overwhelmed is normal, but being afraid to ask for help and step out of that comfort zone is something that we all need to experience to grow.

Creating impact

I recently learnt the scale of species that are becoming or on the verge of becoming extinct. This makes me so emotional and angry at the same time, it sends my heart racing. How have we allowed this to happen? How have we not recognised this sooner so that we could have prevented it? The more I learn, the more I realise that we have created a life that has been self-absorbed as a human race. Land clearing for development is like coming in and bulldozing a complete suburb and not worrying what lives it destroys in its path – we don't do this to humans so how have we allowed this to happen to our wildlife?

As the list continues to grow on our critically endangered, endangered and protected wildlife, it is quite disturbing and only now we are realising if we continue the way we are we will destroy life as we know it. We are creating impact on the ecosystems these animals need to survive which in turn causes a flow-on affect into other areas like our land and waterways.

Having all this information at hand and not knowing the extent of the damage it is causing is disturbing, so I have made a conscious effort to better understand so that I can also educate my children on their surroundings and how they too can contribute to their choices that they want to see in their world.

Giving myself permission to have a voice through storytelling to children in a fun, engaging way to educate and encourage our children to be part of the solutions. Kids don't want to hear about the doom and gloom of their planet, they want to be contributors, and I want to be able to show them how they can be part of the solution through educational games and books.

My vision is to create global impact and to make these solutions accessible.

LEANNE MURNER

Leanne Murner is a global award-winning author and mother to five boys. Her successful educational online toy store is named 5 Little Bears to recognise her commitment to the use of natural products and educating our youth which stems from her passion to show her boys what is possible.

Leanne is widely known for her award-winning series of children's books. Each book educates children on wildlife preservation and regeneration in Australia to align with her vision. She has gained national and global recognition with a swag of awards, including *Franki and the Banksia,* which won the nature category award at the prestigious NYC Big Book Awards 2021, *Oliver and the Eucalyptus Tree* was a finalist in the Book Excellence Awards in the children's education category in 2022 and *My Hollow Home* which took gold the MMH Press Awards for children's education in 2022.

Leanne is passionate about the need for children to be educated through story which will enable them to see how they can contribute to making a global impact in the way they live life and help make better choices for climate change and the preservation of animals, flora and fauna.

Leanne is currently working on a new series that will also have work packs that enhance awareness across of areas she writes about.

LinkedIn: leannemurner
Instagram: @leannemurnerauthor & @5littlebears_aus
Facebook: leannemurnerauthor & 5littlebears.com.au
Website: leannemurnerauthor.com.au & 5littlebears.com.au

TOP TAKEAWAY TIPS

- Things happen for you, not to you; embrace the flow and understand we cannot control every situation. Accept what happens and move on with a positive mindset.

- Many of us overthink or overanalyse situations. Be spontaneous, live in the moment, enjoy and create a limitless life and see what journey you find yourself on.

- Avoid what-ifs, you can't move forward with thinking in the mindset of a negative result.

- Everyone is on their own life journey, and you choose to follow the signs that cross your path.

- The more we can accept that we cannot control life, the more open, intuitive and expansive our thinking will be.

LIKE MOTHER, LIKE DAUGHTER

Oksana Kukurudza

Part 1: Following in Mother's footsteps

I was born the youngest into a Ukrainian immigrant working-class family of twelve children in the medium-sized city of Rochester, New York. My family and I grew up in a small house within the city limits with less than 1,600 sq feet and only 1.5 bathrooms to share between us. Both my parents had very modest jobs – a butcher and janitor. Growing up on farms in rural Ukrainian villages, they lacked access to education and opportunity.

My father could not read or write. He could only sign his name, which he learned from my mother, but he could do self-taught arithmetic. His father spent most of his formative years in prison for murder in Paris, and his mother, as a result, neglected his brother and him, requiring them to rely on the kindness and charity of neighbours to survive.

My mother, an avid reader and dreamer, lost her mother to

pneumonia at a young age, and her father and stepmother took her out of primary school in the third grade to work the farm and take care of the younger stepchildren.

My parents, however difficult their lives were in their homeland, never stopped seeking a better life. When the Nazis invaded their land, which at the time was a part of eastern Poland, they saw an opportunity – and took it. The Nazis were offering work visas to Slavs in occupied territories. My father and mother, separately – at twenty and seventeen years old, respectively – saw this as an opportunity to escape the poverty and unemployment of their villages in 1941, so signed up for work in Germany.

This promise of work, money and freedom soon evaporated; when they arrived in Germany, they had their identity papers confiscated and were sent to slave labour camps with armed guards and dogs patrolling every night.

Years later, in October 2010, I was in Berlin sightseeing for the weekend and happened to come across Berlin's History Museum and Germany's first ever exhibit of Nazism. I was lucky enough to gain entry and see this controversial (because of the lingering white supremacy movements in the country) exhibit for myself. Much of what was displayed was well-known and well debated, but what I remember most from the exhibit was something not well-known and not well debated – the small replica of a Slavic worker slave camp – because it was not only a part of German history but also my family's history. The replica of the camp itself did not look much different from the death camps of Auschwitz-Birkenau I had toured in 1996, leaving me speechless and sick to my stomach. My parents talked so little of their time there. They just said they worked long days in the fields with some food and little or no money. I thought the money was little because inflation was high in Germany at the time. I had no idea it was because the Nazis never paid them for their work and kept them prisoner. I also did not realise how dire their circumstances were while living during World War II under German occupation.

My parents learned fluent German while in the camps, in addition to the Polish and Ukrainian they spoke at home. When they were liberated by Americans, they moved from one camp to another – this time, a refugee camp. As displaced Europeans, with no interest in returning home since it had become a part of the USSR, they were not welcome to stay in Germany. They had to wait it out until a country would welcome them permanently. In and out of the refugee camps, my father took odd jobs as a coal miner and cobbler. He was good at learning the trades.

While in the camps, my parents met and married. They started having children. My father wanted to stay in Germany and had no interest in going abroad. My mother had other ideas. As the dreamer, she somehow had an innate sense to 'think limitlessly'. Even back in her small village of Turka, Poland (Poland at the time but now is part of the Lvivska oblast, Ukraine), she saw the opportunity to leave home and seek more. She even begged and pleaded with her older sister to go, but her sister said no. My mother was different; she sought the new, the better and the different. She never gave up that optimism, even when challenges and barriers were put in front of her. When my parents started having children, my mother applied for asylum with any Western country that would take families – primarily the United States and Australia. Each time my mother had a new child, she would have to reapply for asylum, over and over again. However, this never deterred her. She was as relentless as she was resilient.

My mother's limitless thinking and persistence eventually paid off when the United States, through the Marshall Plan, accepted their asylum status in 1956. They gathered their meager belongings and six children (my mother was pregnant with number seven) from the refugee camp in Frankfurt, and with a Ukrainian-American sponsor in Rochester, New York, identified, boarded an airplane and came to America like many other immigrants before them. My mother dragged my father and children kicking and screaming halfway around the world because she not only thought limitlessly but also was not afraid to go to the limits to achieve it. And I am very much my mother's daughter.

When I was growing up in a modest working-class home, I knew I was poor, but it never really bothered me. I guess it was because I grew up around others who either had less or not much more than I had. Other than watching television, I was never really exposed to much of the wider world around me. I did have a salacious appetite for reading and I believe between that, the attributes I inherited from my mother and good guidance that I was given by my older sister, I began to have little sparks of thinking limitlessly on my own. I remember at a young age seeing my older independent working sister travel to exotic destinations like Florida, California, Aruba and even Australia and wanting to go too. I remember having a huge rush of excitement the first time I flew in an airplane to visit my brother living in Arizona. Where my niece, two years my senior, was homesick when we were in Phoenix and dying to go home, I on the other hand, as an eight-year-old, wanted to stay longer. I dreamt of going to college and living somewhere other than Rochester. I wanted to be a successful professional with enough money to be comfortable. I also considered one day being a writer. I did not know yet how I would do all of those things or what my path would be to get there, but I didn't care. The first secret ingredient to thinking limitlessly is about dreaming, and I always have been a good dreamer.

When I graduated from junior high school as the class valedictorian, I wrote a speech already determined to go to college, with my sights set on the Ivy League. At the time, I had no idea the challenges of getting there. If you were not innately brilliant, a legacy child (family already went there), had millions to donate to the school or could afford to go to the private feeder schools, you had a very small chance of acceptance. At the time, I didn't think in limits – otherwise known as barriers, challenges, reality – I had my dreams, and I was sticking to them. My older siblings always supported me, my teachers always supported me and even the guidance counsellors supported me. I remember a time when I told my ninth grade high school guidance counsellor that I wanted to go to Yale University. Instead of explaining to me that almost no-one at Aquinas Institute in Rochester ever gets into Ivy League schools and that I would probably need to graduate top of my class to be even considered, he pulled out a pamphlet about Yale, gave it to me and told me to go for it. While the first secret ingredient to thinking limitlessly is dreaming, the second is encouragement.

Unfortunately, sometimes dreaming and encouragement are not enough. So, while I was smart, I, unfortunately, was not brilliant or wealthy with connections. This, I learned a bit later when I was considering college. I did extensive research on colleges I felt were within my grasp and segmented them into safe schools, stretch schools and then aspirational. Luckily, through my research and planning, while I was not accepted to an Ivy League college like Yale, I was accepted to a respectable college, Boston University. Not only did this give me the opportunity to gain a solid education, it also gave me the chance to leave home and begin to travel the world, which is another thing people who dream like to do.

THINK LIMITLESSLY

My first trip abroad was to Japan with a good Japanese friend of mine I met in college. During those three weeks in Japan, I felt such culture shock. I absolutely loved immersing myself in the food, history and culture, but I also always knew without my friend nearby, I would have been utterly lost. In 1989, most Japanese people, while having studied English, could not really speak it well – the country was still very much insulated and homogenous. For someone like me visiting Japan who could not read or speak Japanese, it would have been very difficult to navigate travelling in Tokyo, much less the rest of the country, without my friend. However, that experience which could have dissuaded someone else out of their passion for globetrotting just reinforced my determination to continue to travel the world even if I did not know many foreign languages. I believe that is what people do when they think limitlessly. They do not let a bad experience deter them from their goals. They stay persistent to their dreams and aspirations. The third secret ingredient to thinking limitlessly is persistence and not being distracted from your goals.

After college graduation, I went to work in Torino, Italy, on an internship in public accounting. I had not been recruited out of college to work in a public accounting firm, which had been my dream since freshman year of college, but instead of giving up, I found an alternative route to get there – I signed up for an internship in Torino for six months through a global student organisation.

While there, I was contemplating another dream – visiting Greece. I had a passion for Ancient Greece as well as its mythology and being next-door in Italy seemed almost too good to be true. I almost did not go to Greece after my internship ended because I couldn't find anyone to go with me. However, a South African roommate of mine encouraged me to go. She let me know that she ended up in Greece once on her own when her friend cancelled at the last minute. She bought the *Let's Go Greece* book and spent days having fun travelling through Greece on her own safely. Using her example and encouragement, I bought a copy of the book myself, had a great adventure in Greece and have been travelling solo ever since. My most adventurous feat was after MBA school in May of 2001, spending the summer backpacking through Azerbaijan, Armenia, Georgia and Turkey solo on US$30 a day.

In 1993, while I was in college and having my own travel adventures, Ukraine became an independent country from the USSR. My mother, without telling anyone, went to a travel agent and booked herself a trip to Ukraine to visit her sister and her sister's family still there. While both my parents left siblings and stepsiblings back in Ukraine, they never forgot them. While the only communication between the families had to be done through censored letters and pictures, the siblings stayed as close as they could over the years. Both my parents, though money was tight, would collect clothes and other goods to send to their relatives in the Ukrainian SSR. Although our families there only received 30-40% of what was sent to them because USSR custom agents would rifle through every box and take the best stuff for themselves while replacing them with East German knock-offs, my parents would continue to send.

The first my mother spoke of her trip was when she asked my sister for a ride to the airport. Although my mother spoke only broken English, she managed to navigate airline tickets, hotel bookings, visa processing and travelled on her own for her first visit to Ukraine in over fifty years. My mother not only had her dreams and persistence, she also had gumption to think and act limitlessly.

THINK LIMITLESSLY

I do not believe I inherited my mother's gumption. My mother always seemed to be a woman who knew what she wanted, never deviated and was very resolute. She did not need encouragement to stay on her path. In fact, she experienced the exact opposite. Both her father and sister discouraged her from leaving Ukraine but still, somehow, she did it. My father tried to talk her out of leaving Germany, yet she held fast. She was always fearless. While I do believe a secret ingredient of thinking limitlessly is gumption, it is not a requirement for us all. While I remember thinking limitlessly as a child, I was always uncertain if and how I would find the right path to achieve my dreams or goals. Those goals always seemed so distant and impossible to grasp. I was not fearless and did not have the gumption of my mother so how was I going to continue to think and act limitlessly as she did?

Well, while I did not have the same qualities as my mother, I did have something she did not have – I had the love, support and encouragement of family, friends, teachers and even guidance counsellors to give me the courage to pursue my dreams and give me the safe space to plan the steps to get there.

While in college, I learned the way to achieve limitless dreams if one does not have absolute fearlessness, gumption and determination like my mother, was to do a little thoughtful planning instead. I found by thinking in three-to-five-year increments, I could break down a limitless dream into a set of steps with an end target date. By using some planning skills, I could focus my energies on achieving incremental goals that would be much more realistic and help me see the forest through the trees. As I achieved a goal in that three-to-five-year plan, I would take a step back, reassess and course correct as needed to that goal.

A good example of this was one of my childhood dreams to be

a working professional living comfortably. In college, I thought that meant becoming a CPA working for a public accounting firm and working my way up to partner. When I did not get recruited straight out of college, I changed my plan and found an alternative approach. Once I started working for a public accounting firm, I discovered within a few years that I did not want to be a CPA and work my way up to partner at a CPA firm. While I found the 'managing a project' part interesting, I did not find auditing particularly intriguing. Once I learned that about myself, I created a new three-to-five-year plan to help me achieve my end goal of being a successful professional using a different course. My new plan included applying to MBA schools and potentially working in consulting instead. I was accepted to a solid MBA school, Gozuieta Business School, at Emory University.

This time was a bit different from my college experience. I was recruited by a few consulting firms and started working for Accenture. When I started with Accenture, I thought I might stay a few years and then do something different. But it turns out my three-to-five-year plan turned into a twenty-year career in consulting with Accenture where I ended up as managing director (or equivalent of a partner). In this way, I still achieved my goal of becoming a career professional with comfortable means but my path to get there and what kind of professional I would become evolved over time. I had a vision of what I wanted and was not so afraid of the magnitude of that vision because I could break it down into three-to-five-year increments. As a result, I was able to achieve my goal in the long run. Another secret ingredient to thinking limitlessly? Well, that is old-fashioned good planning and project management skills.

Many of my dreams have had practicalities to them. I grew up wanting to be independent, self-sufficient, professional, travel the world and be comfortable. Looking back on my life, I have been able to achieve all those goals save for one. I always wanted to be a writer. I remember back in second grade I wrote my first storybook. It was an anthology of made-up fairytales starting with 'The King Who Was Too Vain'. I wrote a few more stories in the third grade but gave it up soon after. It just did not seem like a very practical pastime for a girl coming from a family with little recreational time on our hands. As much as I moved on early from that dream of becoming a writer, I always kept it asleep in the recesses of my mind. Now, with this current anthology, I am not only spending time thinking about what thinking limitlessly means to me but also using this writing opportunity to pull out that long-anesthetised dream of becoming a writer myself and making it a reality. My life has certainly taken its twists and turns over the years, yet I still have managed to obtain many of the dreams I have wanted since childhood. For me, the last secret ingredient to achieving limitless thinking is the flexibility to realise attaining your dreams and goals may not come in the exact package you thought when you envisioned them, but it does not mean they're any less of a realisation of that dream. I may not be a famous writer yet, or ever. But I now have had the opportunity to write and be published by thinking flexibly.

Thinking limitlessly when we are young is easy because we have not been beaten down by the realities and practicalities of life's survivals. Continuing to think limitlessly throughout our lives and getting to those limitless destinations? Well, that is certainly the greater challenge. Dreams should always be limitless, as should the pathways to get there, and with the secret ingredients of dreaming, encouragement, persistence, gumption, good planning and flexibility, I believe we all have it in us to get there.

Part 2: Following in my own footsteps

I discuss a lot in Part 1 that I have found some secret ingredients to achieving limitless dreams. Many of those ingredients I inherited from my mother, while others I learned and adopted along the way through my own experiences. While I am forever indebted to my mother and father for the nature and nurture attributes they passed on to me, I have also developed my own traits which have helped me chart my own course. While my mother displayed such an independent streak that was so extreme that she would not rely on the encouragement or help of relatives, friends or even her husband, I have realised that I am stronger and bolder with the love and support of those around me.

There have been many times I have experienced challenges and obstacles in achieving limitless dreams. Very few of us have not experienced these challenges and obstacles, and if we have not, then I question if we are thinking limitlessly enough. The right goals and aspirations should be limitless enough that they should not come easily, and they should feel far and out of reach. They should require a multi-year plan to achieve them, and they should be difficult to achieve by yourself.

I have had many of those experiences in my life – coming from a poor immigrant family and being only the second in my family to obtain a graduate degree – whether it was moving away from home for college, working internationally, solo international travel backpacking, a graduate degree, a professional career or single motherhood.

A good recent example of this was deciding in my late forties to become a single mother through the IVF and donor egg process. Originally, I contemplated not returning to work at all and becoming a full-time mother. Once I had my adorable daughter, I decided a couple months after that I wanted to return to work but only on a part-time basis. Luckily, my company was very supportive of me returning and carved out a role where I could still contribute but be with my daughter while she was still quite young. I said that I would reconsider whether I wanted to stay part-time or return to full-time work after her first year.

Returning to work after maternity leave was difficult and full of its own challenges but, just the same, I decided to return full-time. I made that decision despite my friends encouraging me to stay part-time and enjoy the balance between work and raising my daughter that I had achieved. However, for me, it just did not feel like the right choice. While I was working part-time, I felt self-pressure to do more than my part-time status allowed me even though my company was very supportive. I also realised on my own that, while I absolutely adore my daughter and the time we spend together, I was not meant to be a full-time mother. I expect some judgement here on how, as a mother, I would not want to spend twenty-four seven with my toddler, but I realised that wasn't my vision for my life and it also wasn't the greatest use of my best strengths. My babysitter is much better suited to supporting my toddler's needs during the week, and by being personally fulfilled and contributing in the office during the week, I can be the best mother to her during the evenings and weekends. While many working mothers make these choices based on different reasons – preference for work, financial need or self-actualisation – it is not very popular when a mother admits she chooses to work even though she doesn't have to. However, I believe you cannot put thinking limitlessly into practice without being honest with yourself and others. I choose to be a mother because I want to be a mother. I choose to return to work because I need to have goals and accomplishments that fall outside of motherhood. It must be one of the reasons I chose to have a child later in life.

Once I was able to be honest with myself and others about my decision, the actual practice of being a single working mother brought its own set of challenges. How do I manage to juggle longer days at work than I intended without a partner? How do I have enough energy to give my daughter what she needs after those long days when the babysitter leaves? How do I handle the guilt of not always being there for my daughter? How do I accept that the weekends are hers and I will have very little time for myself anymore? I have my good days and bad days working through those experiences and overwhelming feelings. I am able to cope because I know this is what I want and this was my choice. I cope because raising my daughter and working brings enough joy and fulfilment to make it worth the choice. I also cope because while my mother would always do things on her own, I know I cannot. I can think limitlessly and do limitless things because I have family, friends and an amazing babysitter who have helped me along the way. For me, having the support network of a sister who will come stay with me for a few weeks when I have a crazy work schedule or a wonderful friend who will babysit for me when I need to get my hair done or an amazing babysitter who will come on the weekends if I am sick. It is because of them I can be the better me.

Part 3: Following in your own footsteps

I have spoken about my journey and my experiences and how along the way they have allowed me to think limitlessly. I am only one story and there are many stories still of young people who have dreams but are unsure if they should keep thinking limitlessly or surrender to their current limited conditions. I have a lot of nieces and nephews, which is not surprising since I have a lot of brothers and sisters. They often share their own dreams and aspirations with me. I try to be a sounding board of encouragement for them. I make it clear to them that they should have those dreams, they are incredibly important as North Stars to help guide them through life, as well as aspirations they can look forward to accomplishing. However, I am also practical enough to tell them they cannot just think limitlessly, they need to think about the pathways that will help them to achieve those dreams. They should also find family, relatives, friends and colleagues they can trust to share their dreams and work with them to devise a plan to attain them. While they should rely on themselves and not others to define their vision, they should not think they need to go it all alone. Many times, help from others is just what one needs to not only think big but to achieve big things.

The world can feel a bit ugly right now. I sit and write this in the summer of 2022, what I call a summer of huge upheaval and uncertainty. As a global community, we have managed to navigate through two years of COVID-19 deaths, sickness and lockdowns and managed to come out the other side to geopolitical and economic uncertainty. Inflation is on the rise, gas prices are up, the stock markets are down, interest rates are up, the world is heating up and drying out and supply chains are in disorder. There is a war in Ukraine that could result in famine in Africa. With all this uncertainty, one could easily become a cynic about the world and lose hope for our future generations. However, while I try to be a realist in life, I still have the optimism and hope to think limitlessly about our earth's future.

A good example is my parents' homeland. War has been raging in Ukraine for six months now. Ukrainians, while managing to push back the Russians from occupying the entire country, have managed to push the Russians back in the north-east and hold their ground in the east and south even though they are still hugely outmanned and outgunned. Even with these odds and the loss of territory, Ukrainians are not hopeless. They still believe they will overcome those odds, push the Russians out of Ukraine, and continue with an intact country moving towards a democratic and free society integrated with Europe and the West. Ukrainians continue to think limitlessly of a time when their country will be whole again, and they will be embraced as a central member of European nations. If Ukrainians, at one of their most critical and hopeless times in their history, can continue to think limitlessly and hold onto their steadfast dream, then the rest of us should look to them as role models and continue onto our paths to realise our own dreams.

I would ask our future generations today that even with our current uncertainties of economic hardships, climate change and famine, to look to the role model of Ukraine – to hold fast to your dreams even when they seem limited or marginalised by others. Hold onto those dreams and find others who will continue to support and encourage your dreaming. Remember the secret ingredients of thinking limitlessly and achieving those limitless outcomes are: always dreaming, finding encouragement in others, being persistent, using your gumption, planning the pathways to get there and being flexible when course corrections are needed.

This is a time in human history when we must continue to think limitlessly, and it is with that creativity and resolve our future generations will find the right paths to solve these pressing problems.

OKSANA KUKURUDZA

Oksana Kukurudza is currently a managing director working for one of the largest global consulting and technology firms, Accenture, in New York. Oksana has approximately thirty years of professional experience starting in public accountancy, finance and accounting roles and finally, post an MBA from Goizueta Business School at Emory University, management consulting.

Oksana specialises in advising companies on how to transform their finance functions through new operating models, streamlined processes, intelligent automation, change management and technology solutions. In addition, Oksana focuses her time on coaching and mentoring upcoming leaders and developing highly effective teams.

From Oksana's time in consulting, she has authored multiple thought leadership papers on finance post-merger integration, finance operating models and intelligent automation's impacts on the finance function. She has also been cited in articles in the *Journal of Accountancy* and *Global Finance* magazines. She was also a contributing author to *Going Against the Grain*.

Oksana is most proud of her Ukrainian heritage, the time she was able to work internationally, the ninety-plus countries she has visited so far and the number of consultants she has helped rise within the ranks of her firm. She has heard on multiple occasions that she is the person many of her colleagues seek when they are looking for honest and non-sugar-coated feedback and advice. When Oksana is not advising companies or other consultants, she is busy raising her baby daughter, Sofia, travelling the globe for fun, scuba diving, hiking and skiing.

Email: okukurudza@yahoo.com
Linkedin: Oksana M Kukurudza
Instagram: @okukurudza2
Facebook: Oksana Kukurudza

TOP TAKEAWAY TIPS

My key takeaways from my chapter are my secret ingredients to thinking limitlessly and achieving limitless outcomes which are:

- Never stop dreaming. Do not be so cynical that no matter what obstacles life throws at you to think you can't keep dreaming into old age. Life will always throw you lemons. What is important is to keep dreaming even if it means storing those dreams away until there is a time when you are better prepared to achieve them.

- Find advocates to encourage you. When times are tough, look for support wherever you can find it. If someone close to you truly knows you and cares for your best interests, they will be a good sounding board and encourage you towards your goals.

- Be persistent. Goals that require thinking limitlessly do not come easy and you may have to wait your entire life to achieve them. It does not mean the goal is not worth fighting for; often the hard-won dreams are the most fulfilling.

- Gumption. Everyone could use a little gumption or fearlessness when setting out to achieve a goal that is limitless because there may be others out there who will discourage you from your path or try to tear you down. Remember who you are and why you have that dream and then ignore them please.

- Good planning and flexibility. Thinking limitlessly is not the end goal. It is only the beginning of a long journey of self-discovery and accomplishment. Achieving limitless dreams can only come with thoughtful planning and the flexibility to course correct. Sometimes dreams can be achieved in a different manner than you originally intended. Be flexible enough to recognise the same gift even if it comes in different packaging.

SETTLING INTO MYSELF AND MY PURPOSE

Theresa Haenn

The business mantras sound in my head: *Plan your work and work your plan; Teamwork makes the dream work; Your attitude will determine your altitude; You only have one life, make the most of it; Work hard, aim big, Achieve the impossible; Leave the space better than you found it.*

I grew up with the adage that we should always leave something better than when we found it. My mother never defined the 'something'. It could be a space, or activity, or commitment, anything that we start or step into should reflect our good effort and intention to do well. She was teaching us to do our best and to be our best every single day, and her expectations of us were high. Being the first of six children born in quick succession over eight years, I felt that responsibility fully.

This is not a complaint, more a recognition of how my early experiences shaped me to be the woman that I am today.

I was born in a small town in western Massachusetts. Most of the people who lived there worked for small- or medium-sized businesses. The largest employers in the town were the local hospital, the elementary and high schools and the textile mill. Our neighbourhood had lots of children and we all walked the mile or so to school, even in the first grade. Only about half the families living in our neighbourhood had a small, black-and-white television set, but everyone listened to the radio.

Most people had one telephone in the home, most likely in the kitchen or hallway, and in our community, our telephone lines were shared with our neighbours as party lines. We often picked up the phone and heard other conversations on the line. I was around seven years old when our phone line became exclusively ours. Amazing to think of how far we have come over the last fifty-five years. Now we have phones in our pockets instead of in our homes. I miss the camaraderie of the party line though – we could always find someone to talk to when we needed to, even though neighbours across the town knew more than we really wanted them to if they picked up the phone during one of our conversations.

Ever since I was young, I have always felt a strong sense of being the responsible one. I kept my younger siblings busy, got them into the kitchen for dinner, picked up after them in the playroom or helped my mother do what she needed. Being the big sister had its benefits though, because sometimes playing with the babies was fun. They were cute and cuddly, and I was allowed to hold our youngest sister, Roseanne, by myself. I loved to hold Roseanne and I still remember the way she looked at me and smiled. She and I connected; I was sure of that. Mom said her smile was likely gas and that Roseanne didn't understand smiling. I am pretty sure this was the first time I ignored what my mother said.

Sometimes life throws us curveballs, and Roseanne, as sweet as she was, became a curveball for our family. She was born in July with a heart defect and only lived for three months, and some of that time was in the hospital. While Roseanne was with us, I wanted to help my mom, and so I did. It was one of those times when I didn't know why I was doing things, but I just knew that as the big sister, I could do something to help, and so I did.

My mom was energetic, talkative, physical and always moving. My dad was thoughtful, quiet and physical, but I remember Mom moving much faster than he would. If Mom was angry with us, we knew it – loud and clear. My dad let Mom handle most of the disciplinary things, mainly because Mom told us right away when we messed up. Dad would 'talk to us' when he got home, but by then, whatever we did wrong was old news. Dad didn't get angry, but if we went against his expectations, he would be disappointed in us, and that stung more than being yelled at. As a person who felt responsibility, I never wanted to be a disappointment. Mom's anger was fleeting. Dad's disappointment could last for a while.

I felt my dad's disappointment a few times, especially as I got older. He was not someone who would be interested in talking things out. He rarely said that he loved us, and yet, I believe he felt that by taking care of his family he was demonstrating that he loved us. 'Why say it, of course I do,' would be his response. Sometimes, though, we know in our stomach when something is amiss. A curt response to a question, a lack of engagement in conversation or the way one looks at us, speaks much louder than a shout.

My father's disappointment in me felt like shame. Being the firstborn with the sense of responsibility for others from a very young age, I positioned myself to be the one that should step in and know what to do. What I learned over the years is that my sense of responsibility is to myself and to live in my integrity.

It took me decades to realise that living up to someone else's expectation of me is unrealistic. Their expectation is their expectation, and it is okay that it is different from my expectation for myself.

By the time I was thirty years old, my husband and I had lived in Connecticut for a few years and our sons were pre-kindergarten age. My husband's parents were visiting from Philadelphia for the Fourth of July holiday, and they came to see us in advance of a bigger family event. My father-in-law was coming up the stairs of our walk-up apartment, and even though he was moving slowly, he had a smile on his face.

'Hi, Walter, it is so good to see you! How are you feeling?'

By the time he got to the hallway at the top of the stairs, he was a bit winded and flushed, and he said, 'Well, we are glad to see you, and we have some things to discuss.'

Not sure what that meant, but it wasn't the time to ask because the boys burst in and were giving and getting big hugs because they were excited to see their grandparents.

Later that evening, after the boys went to bed, we had dinner, and my father-in-law told my husband and me that the treatment for his cancer was done, and while he felt better, he worried his time was limited, and he wanted to retire. Then THE BOMBSHELL came …

My father-in-law asked my husband and me to buy him out of his inbound call centre (aka answering service) business in suburban Philadelphia. He wanted ME to take over the business and run it. My mother-in-law was smiling in agreement and my father-in-law said, 'Theresa, you are smart, warm, even-tempered, creative, and you will be the best person to manage this.'

The answering service was started in the mid-1950s by my father-in-law's mother who saw a need to provide an out-of-office message-taking service for doctors affiliated with the two local hospitals. Most of the calls were emergencies through the night regarding patients in the hospital, and over time, the service expanded to include message-taking for small businesses in the community such as heating companies, attorneys, etc.

Imagine a person sitting at a switchboard and plugging into a phone line to talk to a caller and take a message; that is how we started in the 1950s. By the time my husband and I bought out my in-laws, the systems were computerised, and we could effectively function as the office receptionist, twenty-four-hours a day for many types of businesses, not just in our area, but anywhere in the US.

When my father-in-law asked me to take over the business, I was shocked. I looked at my husband for his reaction, and he was as stunned as I was. He also looked sad. His father bypassed him and asked me to take over his business. I worried about my husband's feelings of being left out.

My in-laws decided that they wanted us to accept, without any warning or preparation, and presented this as a done deal. They had an answer to every question we asked. It felt like we were teenagers again and being told 'this is what you are doing, end of discussion'.

I felt like I was responsible to help my mother- and father-in-law, and the last thing I wanted to do was be a disappointment to them. Just like my relationship with my father, it was repeating with my father-in-law. UGH!

My mind exploded! On one hand, I was really excited for this challenge. On the other hand, my husband and my own parents were less than enthusiastic. My husband and I resisted being told, yet again, what we would be doing with our life. My parents imagined all sorts of issues that could arise with my husband's family if I took over the family business. I will give my mother credit here; she was right, and I relied on her patience and love when I sought her counsel during some particularly difficult times.

In my default mode of being the 'good girl' and taking responsibility when I was asked to do something, I wondered, *Do we really have a choice?* I debated all the possible scenarios and outcomes for every action from the viewpoint of negative consequences.

What got me excited, though, was the opportunity that this presented. In my optimistic view and excitement for the future I desired, running and owning a business would give me the toehold I needed to be independent. To make my own decisions. To work hard and build a business. I also wanted our sons to see me as an independent working adult, contributing to our family and the community. I was excited for the challenge, even though I felt ill-equipped in understanding the full scope of business matters.

What changed for me was my belief in myself and my commitment to working hard. I already knew how to manage customer service interactions; I started college studying education, I knew I could take what I learned and apply it to managing the staff.

I felt that this was an opportunity to do something impactful. To step into the role as the female leader of the company and find a way to support other women in their endeavors. This has become the purpose for everything I do.

We packed everything up and moved in August, just in time to enrol our sons in school.

Taking action

Even though I had met some of the staff and been in the call centre during previous visits to my in-laws, walking through the door as the new 'boss' was both exciting and nerve-racking. Opening the door, the smells of coffee and cigarette smoke greeted me. I heard about ten to twelve different conversations, with the operators ending calls with a, 'Yes, they will call you when they are back in the office.'

The call centre was set up as three groups of workstations around computer hubs with sound-dampening dividers separating each computer screen.

Helen, the day supervisor, was sitting at her workstation, with her cup of coffee and cigarette next to her. 'It makes a LOT more sense to let us continue to smoke and drink coffee at the station, because it saves time and then we can answer more calls,' she would say.

I knew, though, that coffee and computers do not mix. Especially in tight spaces. Helen did NOT want to hear that she couldn't have her coffee next to her. Even today, when liquids spill on computer equipment, they can be damaged. Back in the 1980s, the systems were even more susceptible to being damaged by liquids, and even worse, anything connected to the computer could also be damaged by the resulting short circuit travelling back to the central hubs.

I encouraged everyone to periodically get up, stretch their legs and get a quick cup of coffee in the kitchen break area. I felt that a brief break every hour or so would be a good stress reliever for them.

Cigarette smoke gave me headaches and irritated my breathing. The smell permeated everything, and I hated the smell of the stale smoke or ashes in the ashtray. The smokers were told to take their cigarettes outside.

The smokers were ANGRY – but the non-smokers celebrated, 'IT'S ABOUT TIME!'

I felt SOOO overwhelmed! Wondering every day if I had what it took to manage this business, ensuring the financial security for twenty-eight families and service quality for our four hundred clients. Could I lead our staff and manage my family while my husband commuted two-plus hours into New York City every day? All the demons in my head questioned everything.

Do I have the skills to do this?

Did I misunderstand what the universe wanted me to do?

Am I certain that I made the right decision?

Do I REALLY understand what I am doing when I am trying to fix the computers?

I could have gone down the rabbit hole of imposter syndrome. Acquiesced to the worry and fear of whether I could actually do this and listen to the negative voices in my head.

I decided to put MY MARK on how I wanted to lead in this business. My mother's advice to leave things better than when I found them started whispering in my head. Most of the people who worked for us were college students or mothers who wanted to be home for their children and needed to work in the evening in an office environment.

Our business was a small family business – truth be told, it was a microbusiness as far as government or business regulations were concerned. We fell below the threshold for many business requirements, so legally, I could offer benefits for our twenty-eight employees that larger businesses couldn't. The late 1980s and 1990s were still in the throes of the women's liberation movement, and one of my goals was to create a working environment in which the women and men who worked for me had a sense of wellbeing and stability on the job.

It would take twenty-five to thirty years before studies would be conducted about wellbeing at work, but I was looking to establish my own sense of wellbeing as a working mother and was using our business to accomplish this. If I was going to create an environment in which I felt a sense of wellbeing by being able to get up and move around or take a quick walk for myself, I felt it was only right to offer it for everyone else too. I had no basis to know, but when I was stressed, the simple act of standing up and moving around or getting some coffee or just washing my hands helped me reorientate my thinking and feel better. Taking a quick walk outside to get fresh air calmed me down and helped me breathe more deeply, which also lowered my heart rate, and I was then able to get back to work. These short breaks sparked the idea that I needed at that moment.

If these simple acts worked for me, then likely they would work for our staff. Taking calls for our clients was often very stressful, because we were their emergency backup, so most calls were important. The speed with which they hit our screens was also stressful, and our staff could take a call from someone angry that the cable was out again, to a medical emergency or food poisoning or even someone who was suicidal. We needed to get up and walk around and change our physical and emotional space after some of these calls. I wanted my staff to be their best for our clients and their callers, and to do that, I knew I needed to trust them to use their time wisely and take the relief they needed when they needed it.

That was a big culture shift for the organisation.

While I stepped into a technologically advanced organisation, we did have staffing difficulties, which is why I wanted to implement wellbeing practices.

I felt connected to our staff because they were working towards a goal, whether that was to support their family financially or put themselves through school. The business books were following

Jack Welch, the former CEO of GE who put forth a philosophy that every company should eliminate the lowest-performing employees, at least 10% of the workforce, every year to keep everyone pushing to achieve high productivity goals. He termed it 'ruthless culling', and that is exactly what it was. Yet, when I looked at my staff, I saw their children, their husbands and knew some of their concerns. They are people, not just efficiency percentages. Our office was small, and our staff stayed with us for a long time, and we knew one another well.

This was one of the surprising lessons of business leadership that I hadn't expected. I felt personally invested to ensure that our business thrived so that we could confidently provide what our staff needed, which centred on their pay and health benefits. If our clients were slow to pay us, we could never be slow to pay our staff, but we were often slow to pay ourselves. I also felt it was important to ensure that our staff didn't know about any difficulty, and that was very hard. In a small office, people seem to know just about everything – or even worse – they imagined that they knew everything that went on.

Important connections

Have you ever stopped to think of all the ways in which we are connected to one another? The seemingly random occurrences that are anything but coincidences and are more like divine interventions.

I had big dreams for myself and our business and struggled with the stress of my everyday responsibilities to ensure our smooth operations, support for our staff and caring for our family. Owning and operating a business around the clock, every day of the year was a big undertaking, and I learned very quickly that most people's holidays were our busiest days. Another business owner that I knew told me once that, 'Your staff will never remember that you were in the office on Thanksgiving, but your family will never forget that you missed Thanksgiving.'

The pressure was fierce and unrelenting. Had I not been focused on creating an environment supporting everyone's wellbeing, I most likely would have sold the business and walked away at the end of the first year. In the professional sense, wellbeing is knowing that our staff have the tools and training to do their work well, that they know I care about them as a person, that other members of the team are working towards the same purpose with the expectation of working at their best, and that they have the opportunity and support for development.

Wellbeing is now a buzzword, with companies talking about ways they encourage wellbeing practices at work by offering certain benefits. Back in the dark ages of the 1980s and 1990s when we owned our business, we were ahead of the curve on these practices, even though we didn't call it wellbeing at the time. I looked at it as if something is good for me, then it is good for the people who work for me. We offered time off, even in the middle of a shift, so that staff could attend to important family needs. We celebrated, and cried, when long-time staff members left to work in a big company because they had the skills and preparation to take on more important roles and manage stressful situations. We offered medical benefits, especially for single moms whose children could finally come off government assistance programs for health care and be on our robust medical plan.

I created a plan to give our staff the opportunity to improve their skills. Prior to my arrival, they hadn't had the resources or training to become excellent in their position, and that saddened me, so I took this as an opportunity to upskill them. Since I had to do a deep dive to learn the intricacies of the computer system myself, I connected with the industry association and volunteered. It was here that one of the top leaders in the association was looking for help to create a training program for staff, and I saw this as a perfect opportunity to be at the table to learn all that I needed to learn from leaders in the field, and then share this knowledge with others.

The timing for this was exactly what I needed and a perfect way for me to deeply learn all that I needed. The best part though was hearing from our clients that they saw a big difference in the quality of our work. Other small business owners who needed us to be their receptionist when they were unable to handle the calls said to me, 'The partnership that we have with you and your staff is one of the things that sustains my business, and my clients appreciate how responsive I am to them, and that is because of you.'

After the Exxon Valdez oil spill in Alaska, we took on an environmental company that cleaned up spills and other disasters and had their response expectations established by the US Congress. We created customised scripts for our staff with decision tree capability depending on the needs of the caller and followed our client's protocol as if we were in their office. The senior leaders told me regularly that our team enabled them to respond immediately and accurately to natural disasters, thereby keeping our waterways safe for wildlife. They even asked me to help them train some of their new employees on how to handle their calls. That was quite an honour.

When my husband and I bought out my father-in-law and I took over the call centre, this gave us the opportunity to refocus the business and make improvements that helped us grow every year until we sold the business, and I began a new phase of my career in the non-profit sector. The call centre was my first experience of leaning into a big challenge, which was often overwhelming, but also good training for many other challenges.

Leap of faith

Taking a leap of faith is risky. Most of my leaps set me on a terrific path to exciting challenges and career adventures. Certainly, I have had failures – some were pretty big and uncomfortable, even embarrassing. I kept going though, knowing that every mistake is a learning opportunity. Every failure is new knowledge of what didn't work and a chance to forge a different path. Even when my confidence was bruised, I worked to ensure that it didn't break me. I never defined myself by what didn't work. I define myself by what can be done and as a person who wants to make this world a better place.

Confidence and purpose are tied closely together. You need one to be able to have the other. On those days when negative thoughts ring in my head and confidence is lagging, I lean on my purpose to provide the boost I need to keep going. It almost seems that for confidence and purpose, one is the battery and one is the engine for our life, and we can use them to recharge when we need it most.

You will be challenged in ways that bring great opportunity to you. It is these moments of hardship that enable you to rethink your plan and move to plan B or C. This is your time to take stock of what you are learning and to gain strength from it. You are gaining valuable knowledge and experience, and these challenges help you to grow.

Others might not share the story I am about to tell you because it describes a shocking change – which, after a thirty-five-year career, was the first time I experienced this shock. My purpose in sharing this is to let you know that sometimes you can bring on your own problems by ignoring the signals and your intuition. I felt I could muscle my way through the challenge and make things work by sheer force of will. That worked for a few months, but truthfully, I knew I needed to face the reality that I put it off for too long.

A few years ago, I accepted a position at a non-profit organisation because I believed wholeheartedly in their mission, and it was a challenge that I felt I was ready to take on. I was told by the CEO before I was hired that I would be able to build my own team because there had been some transition in the department. One fundraising role was filled by a consultant, a grant writer had given notice and a government relations role was open. Of the five positions for staff who would report to me, three were open, and I would have responsibility to hire people to fill out my team and move the organisation away from government funding and focus on individual giving as a priority.

I was excited to start and arrived early on my first day, even before the CEO. When I met with the CEO later that day, I was informed that the consultant had been hired. A few days later the CEO wanted me to give a 'courtesy interview' to a person who had strengths as a liaison for government officials. I did not know at that time that the CEO had already offered this role to the person I was asked to interview. Two of the three roles I was told would be filled by people I would hire, were hired by the CEO, and while they are competent people, they did not fit into the plan the CEO and I discussed for the department during the interview process.

My intuition was screaming, *This is a bad choice! Quit now!* I had stopped interviewing and declined all the other offers to accept this one a month earlier. I had nothing in the pipeline and was worried about being unemployed for a few months until I found another role. I felt stuck. I was operating from a place of scarcity instead of abundance. I thought I could muscle through.

As the weeks became months, eventually our fundraising team came together, and we achieved our financial goals and success in several areas.

The reality, though, was that the CEO had decided he did not want me on the team and became more distant. Frankly, I knew subconsciously that I needed to find a different organisation. I knew I was not functioning the way I should be but was caught up in the details of the work and put off renewing my search for a different position.

The day after my first anniversary, the COO and HR manager came into my office and told me that my services were no longer required. There had been no outright warnings. No bad reviews. I raised more money than we planned, and our fundraising team was working well together. None of that mattered. I was told that they would box my things up and I could leave now. I hadn't even finished my morning cup of coffee. Even though the two who gave me the news were the ones crying, the message was clear: 'Don't let the door hit you on the way out.'

I had never been let go from a position before, and it was really strange riding the train back home at 9:30 in the morning. I felt like I was in a fog and that I was watching myself move through my day like an out-of-body experience. I could have gone into the depths of negativity because I was in shock and not thinking clearly. I took a few days to be angry and sad and honour my feelings around this experience. I have come to learn that if we are going to be able to heal, we have to honour the injury we experience and take the time we need using the process of healing to bring ourselves to a new place of awareness, understanding and self-compassion.

When a door closes on us, I believe there is another one that will open into a new opportunity. I recognised that the mistake

I made was ignoring my intuition and working for someone who lived contrary to my values of honesty and integrity, which meant for me, that I was living against my values for remaining in a position that started with the CEO lying to me.

That honesty and awareness cleared my conscience. I opened my eyes to the many ways in which I could add value in life and in business. That shift in mindset offered clarity on the ways I could make a difference, and I began consulting for an organisation helping young women build leadership capabilities and working for a school that helped children with learning differences.

I learned that it is not about what we are doing, it is how we are doing it that matters. I need to focus on the ways in which I am living my values and making life better for others. I want to leave a situation better from having been there.

Change = opportunity
'Never doubt that a small group of thoughtful, committed citizens can change the world. Indeed, it is the only thing that ever has.' – Margaret Mead, American anthropologist and author.

I always believed I could make a difference. I believe that I have the capability to bring about change – even if on a small scale. But if that small scale is a person in need and I can do something to help, well, that may be a small scale for me, but it is a big scale for that one person. That is one of the reasons I work in the non-profit sector. I am inspired by the courage of the people who receive the benefit of the mission-driven organisations for which I have raised nearly $100 million. Their determination to access services to solve a big problem they face – whether it is homelessness, an illness, an educational need or support – to create a better life for themselves and their families, their persistence and drive are inspiring. Also uplifting are the donors who make all this possible through their gifts. The passion of the women and men with whom I have helped to make generous gifts is both humbling and inspiring. One person can't possibly solve all the problems we have in this world, however, together we can all do our part to make our world a better place to live.

In thinking about what Margaret Mead said and how she lived her life, I reflect on those who inspire me, and outside of people who have a lifetime of achievement, I am most inspired by young people. The ones who see great opportunity for their future. Young women and men who are faced with a challenge or hardship and find a way to create something new and different for themselves and their families.

Just before the COVID-19 pandemic burst forth into our world, I travelled to Tanzania to visit with the leaders and participants in several of the programs for which I am raising contributions. The ones who inspired me the most were the students in an educational program designed to teach them about the agricultural business. The most exciting part of the visit was meeting the students who participated in a competition to earn prize money to implement a creative idea to launch their entrepreneurial business in the sector. The competition was sponsored completely from donations to the organisation and provided $150,000 in prize money for students to test their ideas. Instructors at the institute evaluated the business plans based on financial projections, how the idea would benefit the environment and how the students would be able to market their output in their home community.

Mawazo Milioni had a business plan to grow tomatoes in his home community. To be profitable, he needed to grow about an acre's worth of tomatoes in a traditional planting style. The problem he had to solve is that in his home community, he had space only as large as a small soccer field (about 90' by 60') to grow tomatoes, which would not provide a high enough yield to make the effort profitable. Mawazo's idea was to build a screenhouse, which is a greenhouse with a sheer screen instead of glass, to allow for air flow and sun filtration into the space. Given that Tanzania is just north of the equator, using screens instead of glass for this purpose kept the temperature inside the screenhouse at a similar level as outside.

The screenhouse was about two-thirds the size of a soccer field with a ceiling that was about 15-20' high. Because he needed to grow the equivalent of a full acre's land of tomatoes in this space, Mawazo used wires suspended from above instead of stakes in the ground to enable the tomatoes to grow vertically up to the ceiling instead of spreading along the ground. The smaller space also meant that the water could be conserved and some could be filtered back into the irrigation system. Mawazo harvested the equivalent of 1.5 acres of tomatoes in about 540sq ft, which gave him enough profitability to build two screenhouses for the next season.

Upendo Ngussa had been worried about the health of her mother and grandmother who used wood charcoal as the fuel for their cooking fire. The thick smoke was unhealthy, and the wood burned quickly, which made it expensive to use. Upendo wanted to find a more efficient and healthy way for her family to cook, so she developed a unique briquette that has a high temperature but burns slowly and puts off a low volume of smoke using all natural ingredients.

Upendo developed a recipe and process to create the briquettes from the hulls of rice kernels, which would normally be thrown out, mixed with cassava flour and water, and then compressed and formed into a briquette. These briquettes are a welcome innovation, not just for Upendo's family but for families across

Tanzania. Upendo profitably produced about one metric tonne every week, and her briquettes sold out consistently.

In 2021, Upendo entered an international competition for student entrepreneurs and secured second place in Tanzania, which gave her a small stipend, but more importantly, a business mentor who committed to helping her scale her briquette business and sell across the country. She engaged with a business owner who offered space in his factory in Rwanda so that she could produce her briquettes more cost effectively and in higher quantities, selling them in both countries.

To think that the success of Mawazo and Upendo began because of the generosity of a small group of donors combined with the creativity of educators wanting to change the way young people tested entrepreneurial ideas. All because thoughtful and committed citizens had an idea to change the world for young people.

Philanthropia and humanitas

'I've learned that people will forget what you said, people will forget what you did, but people will never forget how you made them feel.' – Maya Angelou, American poet and author.

What would it mean to think and live limitlessly? Surely, at the top of one's list could be having all the money needed to have and do whatever is desired. While having lots of money would be nice, researchers talk about how contributing beyond our own desires and making a difference for others is the pathway to true happiness and fulfilment. This is one reason why there are more than 1.5 million non-profit organisations in the United States; people see a problem that needs to be solved and they want to find a way to solve it.

The Cleveland Clinic found that, 'Research says that people who give social support to others have lower blood pressure than people who don't. Researchers also say that people who give their time to help others through community and organisational involvement have greater self-esteem, less depression and lower stress levels than those who don't.'

Let's consider how making a difference through philanthropy or volunteerism can be the pathway to fulfilment and happiness.

George McCully wrote that philanthropy comes from two Greek words – *philein,* which means to love and *anthropos,* which means humankind. Philanthropy, then, is the love of humankind. Romans translated the Greek work *philanthropia* into the Latin word *humanitas,* meaning to care about and nourish human potential.

All the stories I have shared are centred on three pillars on which everything happens: the pillar of purpose is at the heart of why the things we do are important; the actions that are taken every single day that come from the purpose; and the relationships made and changed as a result of these actions. At the heart of all this *humanitas,* making a difference for humankind.

Thinking about what Margaret Mead said: 'Never doubt that a small group of thoughtful, committed citizens can change the world. Indeed, it is the only thing that ever has.' This is how it happens, your purpose causes action and involves others who, together with you, make a difference – even for one person. A continuous cycle that grows and grows.

Over the last twenty-five years I built a productive career in non-profit philanthropy and have been inspired by some of the people who wanted to bring about change in their community. What is inspiring about them is that they live with purpose for their work and a strong commitment to a cause. They have a reason for being that underscores and infiltrates every aspect of their life.

I would like to introduce you to a few inspiring people who made a difference for their own family, as well as many other families. Each one became frustrated or scared or shocked by an event that touched them deeply. A sick child. Homeless families. Puppies living in filth and heartless conditions. They took one step towards their goal. Then another step. Then they involved others, and as more and more people joined in, the wave of change became a movement. These people became leaders and knowledgeable spokespersons for their purpose, the cause closest to their heart.

- Lea and Matthew C, a mom and dad who have two daughters with type one diabetes who are strong leaders in the fight to cure the disease, and in their efforts, advocacy and support, they let one of their daughters participate in the first scientific clinical trial open to teens to test a new device designed to automatically measure glucose levels and manage insulin delivery into the body.

- Bob M, the son of two people who each died from Alzheimer's disease, who became an advocate, activist and spokesperson to engage legislators about protecting the rights of people with dementia and especially their caregivers, while seeking funding for research towards a cure and services for families.

- Lee D, who was so angry with the medical community when her son was diagnosed with a disease that she found a way to raise money and launch research into the illness and has since spurred hundreds of millions of dollars into research for that disease as well as other affiliated diseases.

- Betsy L, a woman who provided funding to save puppies from ruthless breeders in puppy mills across the country, built a no-kill shelter and animal advocacy program that was spotlighted by Oprah. She has led the operations teams at the large shelter caring for the animals and helping them be adopted into families, likely saving hundreds of thousands of animals from misery.

- Karen, a woman who, on her way to work every day, passed homeless people and thought of all the houses of worship that are empty during the week and thought, *Can't they be utilised in some way, so moms and their children don't have to sleep in their car or on the street?* Thirty years later, this is a national homeless shelter program and advocacy organisation fighting to help keep people housed.

Each of these incredible people modelled what Matthew told me when he talked about his passion to raise money to fund research to find a cure for diabetes. His philosophy is: 'Why wouldn't you want to give others the opportunity to be involved in bringing about positive change? Why wouldn't you want to give others the opportunity to be part of something big?' Matthew understood the importance of contributing beyond oneself as a pathway to fulfilment and happiness.

And that is what they did. Each one started small with a vision for the future they wanted to create, and day by day, year after year, they persisted, steadfast in taking consistent action towards their vision of what needed to change. Ultimately, each one sparked a movement or a non-profit; they raised not only awareness for their cause, but over the last fifty years, collectively, they continue to raise money for their organisations, which some now have annual budgets of close to $150 million. Because of their efforts, their belief in themselves and their passion to solve a big problem, life has changed incredibly for an untold number of people and animals.

What do these examples mean for you?

Simply that each one started with something they were passionate about. Each one began their journey with a purpose to solve a problem that was important to them. It didn't matter that they didn't have all the information of how to solve this problem when they began. What mattered was that they were going to take every step they felt necessary, even doing things at times that lead to a dead end or trying something that they failed to achieve.

Lee D began her journey in the 1950s when the perception was that women were incapable of taking on the medical community to support scientific research to change the way the disease was managed. Neither Lee, nor any of the others, listened to the people who downplayed their actions or told them that women can't do that, or we don't want 'these people' in our spaces, or it's just a dog or any number of rude, misogynistic statements to try to stop them.

The important thing is that they persisted. Every day. They were unafraid to talk about their dream to everyone – even those who disagreed with them or refused to help. They had no idea when their big thing would happen, but they knew that their efforts every day were going to be part of the solution. That's why they kept going.

Their purpose, passion and *humanitas* propelled them on and they are making life better for many whom they will never meet.

A few points to consider as you begin your journey:

- Think about your purpose as a drop of water in a pond with the ripples extending out well beyond where the drop landed. You are that drop of water, and you are rippling out well beyond what you can see.

- Self-doubt and negative thoughts have the power to keep us from achieving our dreams. Push negative thoughts away – focus on gratitude for what you have and take one action every day that will help you or someone else.

- Coincidences are never coincidental! Think about that. Things that seem out of the blue or random occurrences are likely signs designed to help you notice something important. The fact that you pay attention to these coincidences is important and will give you the insight you need for the best way to act.

- Volunteer. Find a way to give back to your community. Get involved and share your time with a non-profit whose mission aligns with your values, form a team to help raise money for a worthy cause or put on some gloves and grab a rake and garbage bag and help clean your neighbourhood. Whatever you do, it will be helpful for someone who needs it.

- Keep learning something new. There are so many opportunities to learn how to do anything. Absolutely anything. Take, or audit, a class – many colleges offer the opportunity to attend class lectures for free or at a deeply discounted price which is a terrific way to keep learning throughout your life. Join a book club or a mastermind. The library is a free resource to learn a new skill, share your knowledge or even just pick up a book or newspaper you have never read before.

- Become a mentor. Help a person who is younger than you or new in your field and support them as they develop their strength and skills in this endeavor. Share your lived experience with others, especially those who have a different lived experience, so that they can learn from you – and just as importantly, you from them.

- Finally, find the inspiring authors or poets who crystallise your thoughts about what you believe is possible. A poem or phrase that you can keep front and centre and that will guide you through the ups and downs of life, and most importantly, help you think beyond your immediate world and into the wide universe.

Maya Angelou keeps me grounded in how I want to show up every day, and Margaret Mead inspires me to keep pushing to bring about changes that benefit others.

'I've learned that people will forget what you said, people will forget what you did, but people will never forget how you made them feel.' – Maya Angelou, American poet and author.

'Never doubt that a small group of thoughtful, committed citizens can change the world. Indeed, it is the only thing that ever has.' – Margaret Mead, American anthropologist and author.

THERESA HAENN

Theresa F Haenn, co-founder of Aurora Philanthropic, began her career in the non-profit sector in 1999 serving as a major gifts officer, vice-president of development and executive director. Theresa is a strategic leader leveraging her deep understanding of philanthropy and non-profit management to support other non-profit leaders and boards of directors as they set strategic direction to achieve stretch fundraising goals creating impact in the community.

Earlier in her career, Theresa and her husband co-owned a call centre in suburban Philadelphia providing services to businesses, schools and medical practices. The small family business grew more than 300% under their leadership and was recognised as one of the leading companies in their sector.

Theresa utilises strengths-based leadership, creativity and

deep expertise in donor and community-centric practices for her consulting and coaching clients which supports their strategic growth and increased influence.

Theresa earned her MBA from the LeBow College of Business at Drexel University and her BS in Business Management from Rosemont College. Theresa is certified as a CliftonStrengths professional coach from Gallup, from BoardSource as a Certified Nonprofit Consultant, the Coaching Institute, and she has held the Certified Fundraising Executive professional credential from the CFRE Board since 2004.

Email: theresa.haenn@auroraphilanthropic.com
Website: auroraphilanthropic.com
Phone: +1-484-455-4849
LinkedIn: theresa-f-haenn

TOP TAKEAWAY TIPS

- Understand your purpose and how it can support you in your career and dreams.

- Persist – keep going no matter what.

- Practice gratitude for your success, and even more important, your learning opportunities and challenges.

- Trust your intuition and take the time to let your unconscious mind guide you along the path with your values.

- Include others on your journey – they want to help and celebrate your success.

www.ingramcontent.com/pod-product-compliance
Lightning Source LLC
Chambersburg PA
CBHW031252290426
44109CB00012B/549